EUROPE'S BANKING UNION AT TEN: UNFINISHED YET TRANSFORMATIVE

Nicolas Véron

BRUEGEL, BRUSSELS 2024

BRUEGEL BOOKS
Europe's banking union at ten: unfinished yet transformative
Nicolas Véron

© Bruegel 2024. All rights reserved. Short sections of text, not to exceed two paragraphs, may be quoted in the original language without explicit permission provided that the source is acknowledged. Opinions expressed in this publication are those of the author alone.

Edited by Stephen Gardner
Cover design and layout by Hèctor Badenes Rodríguez

Bruegel
33, rue de la Charité, Box 4
1210 Brussels, Belgium
www.bruegel.org

ISBN 978-9-07-891059-6

ACKNOWLEDGEMENTS

The author is extremely grateful for their encouragement and/or substantial feedback to Edmond Alphandéry, Patrick Amis, Victor Amoureux, Ignazio Angeloni, Jörg Asmussen, Giovanni Bassani, Carlo Bastasin, Thorsten Beck, Pervenche Berès, Jesper Berg, Antoine Bergerot, John Berrigan, Ulrich Bindseil, Lorenzo Bini Smaghi, Olivier Blanchard, Paul Bonmartin, Fabien Bouvet, Teunis Brosens, Marco Buti, Per Callesen, José Manuel Campa, Elena Carletti, Pierre-Henri Cassou, Martin Chorzempa, Rebecca Christie, Stijn Claessen, Benoît Coeuré, Vitor Constâncio, Frans van Daele, Stefaan De Rynck, Thomas Dohrn, Andreas Dombret, Marie Donnay, Pierre Duquesne, Wouter Dutillieux, André Ebner, Matthew Elderfield, Colin Ellis, Andrea Enria, Rachel Epstein, Ramon Fernandez, Edouard Fernandez-Bollo, Santiago Fernández de Lis, Paolo Fioretti, Ismael Ahmad Fontán, Ingmar Garrah, Vitor Gaspar, Anna Gelpern, Jörg Genner, Michael Gibson, Charles Goodhart, Christos Gortsos, Sylvie Goulard, Stuart Graham, Anca Grigorut, Pentti Hakkarainen, Martin Hellwig, Marco van Hengel, Ryozo Himino, Gemma van der Hoeven, Levin Holle, Patrick Honohan, Hu Bing, Alexander Italianer, Harold James, Bart Joosen, Patrick Kenadjian, Lars Kroese, Mark Kruidhof, Taneli Lahti, Jacques de Larosière, Rosa Lastra, Sebastiano Laviola, Bastien Le Bars, Jérôme Legras, Alex Lehmann, Ulf Lewrick, Ivo Maes, Stan Maes, Marcel Magnus, Olivier Marty, Nicoletta Mascher, Silvia Merler, Luuk van Middelaar, Eric

Monnet, Emmanuel Mourlon-Druol, Jean-Pierre Mustier, Linde de Nie, Maria Nieto, Marcus Noland, Danièle Nouy, Damir Odak, François d'Orlando, Francesco Papadia, Maddalena Perretti, Christy Petit, Jean Pisani-Ferry, Birger Buchhave Poulsen, Peter Praet, Lucia Quaglia, Mario Quagliarello, Klaus Regling, Olli Rehn, Fernando Restoy, Martin Rhodes, Carolyn Rogers, Stéphane Rottier, André Sapir, Jesús Saurina, Gerhard Schick, Dirk Schoenmaker, Federico Steinberg, Rolf Strauch, Pedro Gustavo Teixeira, Niels Thygesen, Emiliano Tornese, Jean-Claude Trichet, Steffen Ulrik, Shahin Vallée, Herman Van Rompuy, François Véron, Cristina Vespro, Xavier Vives, Harald Waiglein, Johanneke Wetjens, Thomas Wieser, Guntram Wolff, Heinrich Wollny, Pablo Zalba, and Jonathan Zeitlin. Special thanks to Adam Posen, who first suggested the project, and Jeromin Zettelmeyer for their constant support and patience. Giulia Gotti provided excellent research assistance on banks' sovereign exposures. Stephen Gardner's editorial review was invaluable. The text is the author's alone, including any inaccuracies or misjudgements.

CONTENTS

Foreword 3
List of acronyms 5

1 Introduction 6
2 European banking policy before the
   euro-area crisis 10
3 Decision point: the euro-area crisis and the birth of the
   banking union project 28
4 European banking supervision: an old dream come true ... 57
5 Unfinished work: sovereign exposures and
   crisis-intervention framework 87
6 Europe's choice: procrastinate or anticipate 131

References 145
Appendix A: Sample of banks and selected bank-level
data summarised in Tables 1 and 2 156

FOREWORD

Drawing on exhaustive public sources and interviews, Nicolas Véron has written a second draft of the history of European banking union. Someday, after the archives have been opened and economic historians have descended on them, it will be superseded by a third draft. In the meantime, I invite you to read the clearest, most insightful and best-written history of banking union that you will find.

Nicolas's book describes the genesis of banking union, the history and record of the Single Supervisory Mechanism and the tortured and largely unsuccessful attempts to create an equally coherent resolution and crisis-management framework. But the book is much more than that. It is also a documentation of European banking nationalism, a short history of the euro crisis as it affected banks, a concise comparison of the supervisory and resolution frameworks in the United States and the EU, a trenchant critique of the 'three pillar' narrative of European banking union ('supervision, resolution, deposit insurance'), a chronicle of the most recent, fruitless attempts to get banking union unstuck, a lucid analysis of why it is stuck and a concise summary of what is missing.

For all its nuance and historical detail, Nicolas's basic storyline is simple. The original sin of financial fragility in Europe is banking nationalism: the symbiosis of governments and national banking sectors. Banks help fund home-country governments and accept 'state guidance for their lending in matters of national interest'. In exchange, banks and their creditors are offered bailouts in crises. This sounds like a good deal for both sides. But it has awful implications for systemic risk. *Ex ante*, it leads to weak supervision. Once a crisis has been triggered, it leads to vicious feedback loops between the troubles of banks and sovereigns. Common supervision has eliminated an important part of this entanglement. But other aspects – crisis management that remains mostly national and disproportionate exposure of banks to home-country sovereign debt – remain in place. Until these issues are also tackled, financial fragility will not be expunged and cross-border financial integration will remain poor.

Nicolas is in a special position to tell this story. He is to the history of European banking union what Giorgio Vasari was to the history of the Renaissance: a mix of analyst, historian and actor. Like Vasari, he popularised the term whose history he describes (he is careful to avoid the claim that he coined it, giving credit to a 2011 email from the European Commission's Maarten Verwey, who in turn heard it from 'someone'). Unlike Vasari, he is concise and careful about his facts.

Nicolas has had much more influence over the object of his history than transpires in the book. His 2007 Bruegel Policy Brief 'Is Europe Ready For a Major Banking Crisis' contained the first blueprint for European banking union. He credits a Bruegel-International Monetary Fund workshop conducted in February 2007, and particularly the IMF's Jörg Decressin and Wim Fonteyne, for helping him develop these ideas.

As Nicolas documents, European banking union was born in a conference room at Charles de Gaulle airport. But many of the ideas that went into it can plausibly be said to have been born in a Bruegel conference room. As the current Director of Bruegel, it gives me great pleasure to close this loop by publishing Nicolas's splendid short history.

Jeromin Zettelmeyer
June 2024

LIST OF ACRONYMS

AML	Anti-money laundering
BRRD	Bank Recovery and Resolution Directive
BSSC	Banking Supervisory Sub-Committee
CDG	Charles-de-Gaulle airport
CEBS	Committee of European Banking Supervisors
CMDI	Crisis Management and Deposit Insurance
CRR	Capital Requirements Regulation
EBA	European Banking Authority
ECB	European Central Bank
EDIS	European Deposit Insurance Scheme
ESM	European Stability Mechanism
FDIC	Federal Deposit Insurance Corporation
IMF	International Monetary Fund
IPS	Institutional Protection Scheme
RBS	Royal Bank of Scotland
RTSE	Regulatory Treatment of Sovereign Exposures
SRB	Single Resolution Board
SREP	Supervisory Review and Examination Process
SRF	Single Resolution Fund
SRM	Single Resolution Mechanism
SSM	Single Supervisory Mechanism
TFEU	Treaty on the Functioning of the European Union

1 INTRODUCTION

The banking union is the European Union's project to integrate banking-sector policy in the euro area[1]. Following decades of debates, and momentous decisions taken in 2012, it became a reality in 2014, fifteen years after the euro itself, when the European Central Bank (ECB) assumed authority as banking supervisor.

Therefore, 2024 marks not only the quarter century anniversary of the euro, but also the tenth anniversary of European banking supervision, the main initial achievement of banking union. This volume revisits the banking union's genesis, describes and assesses its development so far, and discusses the missing pieces and prospects for eventual completion.

There is a strong case, corroborated by some of the principal participants in the 2012 breakthroughs, that the decision to grant the ECB a banking supervisory mandate was instrumental in enabling its decisive action in the summer of 2012 that ended the most disruptive phase of the euro-area crisis. This alone brought incalculable benefits to Europeans, as well as to the global financial system. The resulting

---

1   The geographical scope of the banking union is broader in principle than the euro area, and as of 2024 includes Bulgaria, which has not yet adopted the euro. The link between banking union and the euro, however, is critical and is detailed in chapter 3.

micro-prudential supervisory framework[2], centred on the ECB, is essentially complete, resulting in much-improved protection of the euro area against financial instability than during the first decade and a half of monetary union. So far, European banking supervision appears to have been effective, in comparison both with the previous regime of national supervision in euro-area countries and with international peers, notably the United States where severe gaps in banking supervision were observable in the regional banking crisis of March 2023.

In the area of crisis management and resolution, by contrast, progress towards a consistent framework has been halting and remains inadequate. The reasons for this include the interrelated challenges of concentrated sovereign exposures, reluctance to establish a European deposit insurance system and major differences between national preferences in terms of the trade-offs between rescuing ailing banks with public money or imposing financial burden-sharing on private-sector claimants.

The banking union's supervisory framework, beyond its short-term effect as enabler of the ECB's critical decisions in the summer of 2012, makes the euro area – and by implication the EU – much stronger and more resilient than it was before. However, the incomplete crisis management and resolution framework, which implies obstacles to full banking-market integration, carries significant costs in terms of both lost EU growth potential and fragility in certain crisis scenarios, even though it does not create an immediate emergency. The likelihood of concrete advances towards banking union completion appears deplorably low in the short term, unless a crisis generates renewed policy impetus.

---

2 Contemporary financial regulatory parlance makes a distinction between micro-prudential supervision of individual regulated financial institutions and macro-prudential oversight of the financial system as a whole. European banking supervision is currently focused on the micro-financial component.

None of the obstacles to banking union completion are intrinsically insurmountable, however, even in those EU countries where they appear to be most powerful.

Inevitably given the subject matter's scope and complexity, I do not cover extensively certain important banking union-related topics, even though my analysis and recommendations are provided with due awareness of them. These include, but are not limited to, macroprudential, emergency liquidity and financial-conduct policy frameworks (including protection of bank clients against mis-selling and anti-money laundering policy, both of which have prudential implications); bad banks; financial sanctions; whether non-euro-area countries might join the banking union voluntarily[3]; and the interplay between banking union and the sequence of events that led to the exit of the United Kingdom from the EU[4].

The methodology used for the preparation of this volume is similarly incomplete. I have relied on numerous conversations and interviews with a wide range of interlocutors, but even so have likely missed important perspectives. The relevant academic and policy literature turned out to be already too vast to be reviewed exhaustively[5]. I

---

3   That question was addressed near-simultaneously in December 2019 by high-level reports in Denmark and Sweden. No significant developments, however, have occurred since then. See Government of Sweden (2019) and Danish Ministry of Industry, Business and Financial Affairs press release of 19 December 2019, 'Report from the Working Group on possible Danish Participation in the Banking Union,' https://www.eng.em.dk/news/2019/dec/report-from-the-working-group-on-possible-danish-participation-in-the-banking-union.

4   A causal link between banking union and Brexit has been suggested both *ex ante* (eg Barker and Parker, 2012) and *ex post* (eg Rogers, 2017).

5   Banking union has become a specifically identified field of study in the last decade, primarily by legal scholars, to a lesser extent political scientists, and even less so economists. Reference publications include Busch and Ferrarini (2015), Lo Schiavo (2019) and Teixeira (2020). The PhD thesis by Schäfer (2017) relied on numerous interviews with key players, many of whom corroborated my own findings. De Rynck (2015), Nielsen and Smeets (2018) and Angeloni (2020) stand out among in-depth accounts by past protagonists.

conducted no archival work of my own, both because of my lack of experience in that field and because few if any archives are so far open to investigation of recent events[6].

---

6 For the early period including the negotiation of the Maastricht Treaty, much archival work is available, some of which is referred to in chapter 2. I am especially grateful to Emmanuel Mourlon-Druol for generously sharing parts of his book manuscript ahead of publication (Mourlon-Druol, 2025).

2 EUROPEAN BANKING POLICY BEFORE THE EURO-AREA CRISIS

The relationship between Europe's banks and sovereigns goes back a long way. It rests on multiple historical and institutional legacies that outside observers often find difficult to comprehend, and that many Europeans are also unaware of. Most of today's European banks trace their origins to the nineteenth and early twentieth centuries, the period of emergence of nationalism in its modern form. Many were created in a context of national and/or colonial development projects, and occasionally participated in the financing of intra-European warfare. A number of these banks were directly or indirectly sponsored by local or national governments.

By contrast, in the United States, bank creation has largely been a bottom-up, entrepreneurial phenomenon, even though it was subjected to general regulatory requirements at a comparatively early stage. A stable coalition during most of the nineteenth and twentieth centuries inhibited the ability of US banks to expand nationwide and exercise political influence at the federal level (eg Calomiris and Haber, 2014, chapter 6). In the country's early decades, there existed a financial nexus between banks and government at the level of individual US states, but that direct linkage largely disappeared in the course of the nineteenth century (Gelpern and Véron, 2018).

In return for national government patronage, European banks often found it natural or inevitable to facilitate state financing, to direct credit to government-favoured companies, sectors or projects, and to support government policies and strategies domestically and abroad. The ways these relationships formed and developed varied widely across European countries. In many cases, they meant lower benefits for savers and other stakeholders in the banking system, a pattern that economists refer to as 'financial repression'. Conversely, 'banking nationalism' is an imprecise but useful umbrella expression to summarise the inclination of governments to protect and promote national banking champions in the history-laden European context. Whereas the relationship between European banks and governments in the last century or two has been complex and rarely one of full alignment, it has been generally closer than arm's length[7].

Early debates and initiatives on European banking policy integration

In the initial phases of European integration, negotiators and legislators displayed no appetite to disrupt these national legacies. The Treaty of Rome (1957) included specific provisions requiring unanimity among member states for "*measures concerned with the protection of savings, in particular the granting of credit and the exercise of the banking profession*" (Article 55). This made it more difficult to harmonise banking legislation than for most other service sectors for which qualified-majority voting was the rule (Maes, 2007, page 27). The European Commission's first banking policy integration initiative, which started in 1965, stopped short of centralised prudential supervision, and even so had petered out by the early 1970s (Mourlon-Druol, 2016). A 1973

---

7   There does not appear to exist a reference in-depth comparative analysis of bank-sovereign linkages across European countries with a long historical perspective, let alone a comparative study of these linkages in Europe and the United States. Cameron (1967) and Kindleberger (1993) provided a number of examples; see also Hellwig (2014), page 26.

directive on freedom of establishment in the banking sector changed little, as it did not attempt to address divergent national regulatory requirements and the cross-border obstacles linked to national capital controls[8]. Following these early experiences, the European Commission adopted a decidedly incremental approach to banking sector integration, its first step being the so-called first banking directive of 1977[9].

Significantly, banking industry representatives had generally less favourable views of European-level policy integration than their counterparts in other sectors such as manufacturing. They did not engage in any large-scale cross-border consolidation, opting instead from the late 1950s onwards for loose alliances or 'clubs' of banks from different countries, intended to generate synergies while not fundamentally putting into question the principle that each bank would retain its national identity (Drach, 2021). In a 1981 position paper, the European Banking Federation said that "[n]*ational differences were to be preserved*" (Drach, 2020, page 780). In the late 1980s and early 1990s, the liberalisation of capital movements and the European Commission's single market programme coincided with more positive attitudes to European banking integration. Even then, however, and unlike in manufacturing, the banking industry showed little enthusiasm for harmonisation initiatives, and preferred to advocate softer options of mutual recognition that preserved national regulatory differences and the protection of national banking champions (Drach, 2020).

Moving from regulation to prudential supervision, a number of pan-European bodies were created to foster cross-border coordination. In a recurring pattern, each of these initiatives raised initial hopes among the officials directly involved that they might result in a future integrated

---

8   Council Directive 73/183/EEC of 28 June 1973.
9   Council Directive 77/780/EEC of 12 December 1977.

supervisory framework. But such hopes, which were only expressed in private, typically disappeared after the first few meetings, and the principle that supervisory authority rested exclusively at the national level remained firmly defended.

First came the Committee of Governors, created in 1964 on the initiative of finance ministers, in which the heads of the European Community's national central banks met monthly on neutral ground in Basel. This committee later played a pivotal role in the creation of the ECB, but initially had no direct impact on supervision, if only because that role belonged to the central banks in only three of the six countries[10]. Second and separately, in 1972, the member states' prudential authorities took an initiative of their own to establish a contact group that also met regularly, generally referred to by its French name the Groupe de Contact. Third, in 1978, the European Commission fostered the creation of a Banking Advisory Committee (BAC), bringing together senior officials from each country's central bank, supervisory agency (if it was separate from the former) and finance ministry, with typically one meeting every quarter. Fourth, in 1988-1990, frustrated by the European Commission's reluctance to further empower the BAC, the Committee of Governors established within itself a Banking Supervisory Sub-Committee (BSSC), meeting ahead of the BAC with a permanent secretariat provided by the Bank for International Settlements in Basel (Mourlon-Druol, 2025, chapter 9).

Expectations of future supervisory integration were expressed early on, though only confidentially, with the understanding that the matter would be too controversial to be broached in public. Conversely, from

---

10   Both Belgium and Germany had banking supervisory commissions that were separate from the central bank, and Luxembourg, in monetary union with Belgium, had no central bank at all. By contrast, in France the banking commission was practically under the control of the central bank, and in Italy and the Netherlands the central bank was directly in charge.

early on, the principled opposition of at least some member states was stated explicitly behind closed doors. Thus, in December 1973, one of the members of the Groupe de Contact wrote to his peers: *"Although it may still seem rather far away, one could envisage our informal 'Club' as the nucleus of a future European Bank-controlling authority"* (Goodhart, 2011, page 15). But in 1974, the Bank of France was clear that the Groupe should not receive delegated powers of banking control (Drach, 2019, section 1).

Similarly, in 1978, a European Commission official wrote in internal correspondence that one of the objectives of creating the BAC was *"to provide a forerunner of an EEC* [European Economic Community] *Supervisory institution."* But later in 1978, another Commission official noted in the runup to the BAC's inaugural meeting that the *"leading personalities in the* [French Finance] *Ministry have most of the time taken a rather sceptical view of EEC banking coordination at least when it comes to any decision implying a certain transfer of supervisory powers"* (Mourlon-Druol, 2025, chapter 6). Following the same pattern, in May 1990, the secretary of the BSSC wrote to the sub-committee member from the Bank of England that the BSSC was *"seen as the fore-runner to the policy-making directorate of a Banking Supervision Division of the ECBS",* the latter acronym being then used for what would become the ECB (Mourlon-Druol, 2025, chapter 9). But as detailed below, the creation of the ECB did not initially provide for a strong banking supervisory function within the institution.

During these early decades, the connections between a single market for banking services, monetary integration and banking policy integration were often clearly identified from an analytical standpoint. For example, the European Commissioner for Budget and Financial Control and Financial Institutions, Christopher Tugendhat, noted in 1978 that it *"would be easier to implement a common monetary policy if we had banking systems supervised according to equivalent common standards, and eventually of similar structures. Moreover, to the extent to which the European Monetary System* [which would be established in 1979] *gives rise to more capital liberalisation, we have to make sure to be able to monitor the actors in this forthcoming common capital market, i.e. the European credit institutions, on the basis of equivalent rules."* In 1982, Tommaso Padoa-Schioppa, by then the director-general for economic and financial affairs at the European Commission, noted with reference to Europe's financial system: *"To the extent to which there therefore is a need for control and supervision, the question arises of determining the appropriate level at which they should be exercised, and in this regard there is a solid case for operating them at a Community Level"* (Mourlon-Druol, 2016, pages 920 and 923). In 1991, at a time when the negotiations on monetary union were already underway but their outcome was not yet known, American officials reflecting on lessons from the previous decade's US savings and loan crisis lucidly identified the risk of a supervisory race to the bottom resulting from the interaction between European single market integration and supervision remaining at the national level[11].

---

11   Their contribution to a symposium in Berlin deserves to be quoted at length: *"Obviously, decisions about where to locate banking activities depend on many factors. However, differences in supervision could be one of those factors affecting E*[uropean] *C*[ommunity] *banks. Banks could choose to establish their headquarters (or separately capitalized subsidiaries) in any of the 12 countries based on perceptions of regulatory strictness – or the lack thereof. While it is hard for us to judge from the outside, it is possible that regional interests could also lead to what in the U.S. has been called 'competition in laxity' among the bank regulators. In order to spur economic development within their national boundaries or to lure headquarters jobs in financial services, some nations may be inclined to use concessions in the rigor or cost of supervision as an incentive. […] This could have a serious effect on bank safety and soundness in the EC if regulatory convergence results in increasingly lax supervision"* (Swaim and Wessels, 1991, pages 24-25).

Monetary union and the Maastricht Treaty's 'enabling clause'
While European monetary union had been a matter of policy discussion since at least the early 1970s, its effective starting point was the so-called Delors Committee report, delivered in April 1989. That text, however, was distinctly timid on banking supervision. The report's recommendation that the European System of Central Banks "*would participate in the coordination of banking supervision policies of the supervisory authorities*" (Delors, 1989, page 22) implied that supervision would continue to be exercised at national level[12]. The supervisory challenge, however, was subsequently taken up by the Committee of Governors and its Banking Supervisory Sub-Committee (BSSC). On the basis of the Delors

---

12 This appears not to have been for lack of consideration of supervisory matters in the Committee's proceedings, but rather for lack of consensus on a more forceful approach. The Committee's rapporteurs, Gunter Baer (a German official at the Bank for International Settlements) and Padoa-Schioppa, had referred to supervisory issues in one of the two documents they drafted ahead of the committee's first meeting, suggesting that a single currency should be associated with centralised banking supervision (Vianelli, 2022, page 321). During that preparatory work, Bundesbank President Karl-Otto Pöhl advocated granting the future ECB an active, albeit non-decision-making, role in banking supervision similar to that of the Bundesbank in Germany: "*The European central bank* [...] *should be closely involved in day-to-day banking supervisory activities*" (van den Berg, 2005, page 274). In January 1989, Dutch central bank governor Wim Duisenberg proposed that the future European System of Central Banks "*will be responsible for the formulation of banking supervisory policy at the Community level and co-ordination of banking supervisory policies of the national supervisory authorities.*" This text was included in a next iteration of the working draft of the Committee report, but watered down to the above-quoted wording in subsequent rounds (van den Berg, 2005, page 278). Committee member Alexandre Lamfalussy was among those who tried to raise the supervisory challenge (Maes, 2017, page 19). Another Delors Committee member, the economist Niels Thygesen, mentioned the concern of some participants, ostensibly the central bank governors from Germany and possibly also Denmark, that granting the future European central bank a supervisory mandate "would inevitably lead to onerous political oversight and constitute a threat to [its] autonomy" (Enderlein and Rubio, 2014). Jacques de Larosière, French central bank governor at the time and a member of the Delors Committee, later recalled: "*We did not spend much time in these issues* [of financial stability and banking supervision], *also because banking supervision might have been a divisive issue, as there were significant differences in the responsibilities in this area of the different central banks*" (Maes and Péters, 2021, page 119).

Report, the Council[13] in April 1990 effectively mandated the Committee of Governors to prepare a draft statute for the future European Central Bank. In November 1990, the Committee of Governors, building on the BSSC's work, agreed to propose that the ECB might be explicitly granted a banking supervision role: *"The ECB may formulate, interpret and implement policies relating to the prudential supervision of credit and other financial institutions for which it is designated as competent supervisory authority"*[14].

In contrast to their central banks, however, the most influential national governments were unwilling to relinquish what they saw as an essential tool to leverage the banking sector for their policy purposes – in other words, financial repression. Looking back at the formative period of the euro, Erkki Liikanen, at the time the Finnish ambassador to the European Communities[15], observed that *"the only missing part was that you should have had the banking union, bank supervision at European level, bank resolution, deposit insurance. That was discussed at the time. But member states did not want it, they were stating, we can handle our banks, we know they are in good shape"*[16]. In a clear reference to the direct control exercised by the German finance ministry over its bank supervisory

---

13   In the confusing semantics of European institutions, EU countries meet in the Council (full name Council of the European Communities until 1993 and Council of the European Union since then), to which the rest of this volume refers as the EU Council for readability. This Council is not to be confused with the European Council, the highest EU political body consisting of the EU heads of state and government, meeting formally four times a year, chaired since late 2009 by a full-time European Council President. The Council of Europe is a separate, non-EU institution in Strasbourg, and plays no significant role in the banking union story.
14   James (2012b, page 292) wrote that the Committee of Governors put this text in square brackets to account for the Bundesbank's reservations, but that claim appears to result from confusion with an earlier draft (van den Berg, 2005, page 281; Mourlon-Druol, 2005, chapter 9).
15   Liikanen was subsequently a European Commissioner, then governor of the Bank of Finland. At time of writing, he is chairman of the board of Bruegel.
16   Tim Gwynn Jones, 'In the Room' podcast, December 2022, https://uk-podcasts.co.uk/podcast/in-the-room-1/.

authority, European Commission official Alexander Italianer, who later became Commission Secretary-General, noted drily that a European-level responsibility for financial stability *"would also mean that some finance ministries would see their prudential powers transferred to the ECB. This presumably partly explains the difficulties in reaching agreement on the role of the ECB in the prudential area"* (Italianer, 1993, page 87).

At an early stage of the process in August 1989, the French Treasury expressed its position that any supervisory role for the future ECB *"should be kept out of the negotiation"*. In May 1991, during the first round of formal discussion of the draft statute produced by the Committee of Governors, the French Treasury again led the charge against such a role, with the support of its British and German counterparts and despite dissenting advice from the Bank of France[17]; smaller member states that favoured ECB supervision did not form a consistent coalition and were in any case no match for the combined political weight of the three largest countries[18]. Nevertheless, the Dutch team that took over the rotating Council presidency during the last semester of negotiation (second half of 1991) managed to forge an agreement on an 'enabling clause' that

---

17   Larosière had argued to the Treasury in January 1991 that *"the participation, as necessary, to the definition, coordination and execution of policies relative to prudential control and the stability of the financial system"* was an *"important element of the content of monetary union"* (Mourlon-Druol, 2025, chapter 9). An in-depth study of the drafting process concluded: *"Quite clearly, the Trésor took another position than the Banque de France, presumably because the Trésor had only reluctantly accepted the independence of the ECB and now the aim was to give the ECB no more powers than necessary"* (van den Berg, 2005, page 283).

18   During an important meeting on 6 November 1991 that examined the Dutch Presidency's proposal for the enabling clause, France, Germany, Luxembourg and the UK voted to delete the suggested text entirely, whereas Portugal, Italy, Spain and Denmark voted to retain or strengthen it (van den Berg, 2005, page 286). The European Commission was mostly opposed to a supervisory role of the ECB, apparently for bureaucratic reasons. In a June 1990 Commission note on the matter, it was argued that *"there is no reason to suppose that central supervision by the Eurofed [sic] will be more efficient or less likely to failure than supervision by the national banking authorities"* (Mourlon-Druol, 2025, chapter 9).

preserved the possibility of a future supervisory role for the ECB, albeit under an onerous condition of unanimity[19]. The ministers approved that clause at their meetings on 1-3 December 1991. As a consequence, prudential supervision did not have to be discussed at the final meeting of the European Council that finalised the text of the treaty on 9-10 December 1991 (Mourlon-Druol, 2025, chapter 9). That meeting was held in the Dutch city of Maastricht, for which the treaty became known as the Maastricht Treaty.

The enabling clause was thus enshrined in article 105(6) of the Maastricht Treaty. Following subsequent revision, that clause has been referred to since 2009 as article 127(6) of the Treaty on the Functioning of the European Union (TFEU). It stated: *"The Council may, acting unanimously on a proposal from the Commission and after consulting the ECB and after receiving the assent of the European Parliament, confer upon the ECB specific tasks concerning policies relating to the prudential supervision of credit institutions and other financial institutions with the exception of insurance undertakings"*[20]. As we shall see, in mid-2012 this convoluted language was found sufficient as a legal basis for essentially the same arrangements as the Committee of Governors had suggested

---

19 The Dutch Presidency's drafts in September and October 1991 suggested a qualified majority decision, but a shift to unanimity was the only way to salvage the enabling clause in the November meeting referred to in the previous footnote (van den Berg, 2005, page 286). Frudiger (2022) detailed the policy entrepreneurship of Dutch policymakers, and especially of Wim Duisenberg, in the negotiation, including their active promotion of a supervisory role for the ECB. The exclusion of insurance from the ECB's potential supervisory scope under the enabling clause also came from the Dutch team before being accepted by the other member states (Smits, 1997, page 356, footnote 145; see also van den Berg, 2005, for details on this issue). Enria (2020b) asserted that the enabling clause owed to the *"direct intervention"* of Padoa-Schioppa, who at the time was Deputy Director-General of the Bank of Italy and member of the BSSC.

20 The reference in this text to 'assent' of the European Parliament was watered down to a mere consultation when the article's wording was revised in the Lisbon Treaty, signed in late 2007. The rest of the article was not modified substantially.

in their draft ECB statute of late 1990, as regards effective supervisory authority, if not policy formulation.

In the immediate aftermath of the adoption of the Maastricht Treaty, the absence of an integrated banking policy framework to match monetary unification was not lost on observers. Writing in 1992, veteran financial historian Charles Kindleberger cited "the regulation of banks" as the first of "a series of questions to be resolved on the road to European monetary and financial integration" (Kindleberger, 1993, page 446). Legal scholar Rosa Lastra observed: *"the lack of a clearly defined banking supervisory role for the ESCB* [European System of Central Banks], *with a 'single banking license' in place, could have disruptive effects should there be a systemic crisis"* (Lastra, 1992, page 513). Financial economist Alberto Giovannini wrote: *"one suspects that a half-complete monetary union, not accompanied by reforms of institutions like the payments systems and banking supervision, might give rise to efficiency costs that can easily offset the estimated benefits from the introduction of a single currency"* (Giovannini, 1993, page 226). Economic historian Barry Eichengreen predicted: *"National* [supervisory] *authorities will be pressured to extend regulatory advantages to domestic banks […] But many of the costs of competitive deregulation, in the form of financial instability, will be incurred by the* [European] *Community as a whole"* (Eichengreen, 1993, page 1344)[21]. Such lucid warnings, however, went mostly forgotten in subsequent years.

---

21   It is of note that, in most of the discussions documented here, considerations of banking supervision were not matched by discussions of similar intensity about crisis management and resolution. In effect, most (though not all) participants appear to have shared a belief that solvency crises should and could be avoided with high-quality supervision. Swaim and Wessels (1991) and Vives (1992) represented rare exceptions to this pattern, and were presumably influenced by their direct knowledge of, respectively, the US savings and loan crisis of the 1980s and the Spanish banking crisis of the early 1980s.

From Maastricht to the 2007 financial crisis

The linkages between banking market integration, monetary unification and banking-sector policy were debated at length in the 1960s, 1970s, 1980s and early 1990s. By contrast, these linkages barely featured in the numerous arguments about the design of Europe's economic and monetary union and its prospects between the immediate aftermath of the Maastricht Treaty and the outbreak of the great financial crisis in 2007. A survey of US economists' largely sceptical views of the euro between 1989 and 2002 mentioned banking-sector concerns only once (Jonung and Drea, 2009). That was a 1999 polemic that forecasted the euro's impending collapse and along the way identified future banking-sector bailouts as one of several drivers of future unsustainable government deficits in France and Italy, based on the then recent cases of France's Crédit Lyonnais in 1994-1995 and Italy's Banco di Napoli in 1995 (Calomiris, 1999).

In other words, there were many predictions of doom for the euro during that period, but the bank-sovereign vicious circle that nearly broke the monetary union in 2011-2012 was not one of the identified weak points[22]. Nearing the end of his term as ECB President in October 2019, Mario Draghi reflected that *"not unlike the ecological crisis, the euro area crisis has uncovered multiple feedback loops that were previously not well understood, for instance between sovereigns, banks and firms"* (Draghi, 2019).

---

22 Calomiris's scenario, aside from getting the forecast wrong, identified one component of the bank-sovereign dynamics but not the full circle, since his analysis did not envision that greater fiscal stress would in turn undermine banking sector soundness. One of many other predictions of euro-area collapse published at that time was predicated on a scenario in which the ECB would be prematurely granted supervisory authority under the Maastricht Treaty's enabling clause in 1999, and would find itself unable to exercise this authority as effectively as national supervisors used to, thus contributing to the buildup of financial risk in the euro-area banking system (Lascelles, 1996). This scenario is the exact opposite of what actually happened in the 2000s.

In terms of policy developments, there were some efforts towards greater harmonisation of the banking regulatory framework, but they took the form of directives as opposed to regulations, such as the Banking Directive of 2000 and the Capital Requirements Directive of 2006[23], meaning that these texts still needed to be transposed into the legislative order of each member state, with resulting differences across EU countries. A few incremental changes also happened in EU supervisory architecture during that period, but without fundamentally altering the principle of national supervision.

As the ECB started operations in 1998 in Frankfurt, it established an internal Banking Supervision Committee, composed of euro-area countries' national banking supervisors and central bankers, with the aim of facilitating cross-border cooperation and the exchange of relevant supervisory information. Just as the ECB had (indirectly) succeeded the Committee of Governors, its Banking Supervision Committee was the heir to the Committee's BSSC. The ECB subsequently attempted to influence choices over national supervisory architectures in individual EU countries, arguing that national central banks should be granted prudential supervisory authority over banks to achieve synergies with their core roles of oversight of financial infrastructure, macro-prudential monitoring and liquidity operations in the event of crises. The ECB added that such arrangements would reinforce the independence and professionalism of banking supervision and the handling of systemic risk, and downplayed counterarguments based on considerations of potential conflicts of interest, moral hazard and excessive accumulation of power by central banks

---

23   Respectively Directive 2000/12/EC of 20 March 2000 and Directive 2006/49/EC of 14 June 2006. In EU legal parlance, a 'regulation' is an EU legislative act that is directly applicable in all EU countries upon enactment at EU level, as opposed to 'directives,' which are also EU legislative acts but which set minimum standards that countries must comply with by enacting further national legislation, known as transposition.

(ECB, 2001). That position was instigated, among others, by Tommaso Padoa-Schioppa who joined the ECB as Executive Board member at the institution's inception in June 1998 (Bini Smaghi, 2011; De Rynck, 2014). Padoa-Schioppa was also an early proponent of the full harmonisation of EU legislation on bank prudential requirements, for which he coined the expression "*single rulebook*" (Padoa-Schioppa, 2004).

The ECB was distinctly unsuccessful in its lobbying effort, however. This was most obviously illustrated by the establishment in 2002 of BaFin (*Bundesanstalt für Finanzdienstleistungsaufsicht*) as Germany's integrated financial supervisory authority, which like its predecessor was placed under the close oversight of the finance ministry but separate from the Bundesbank[24]. In 2004, the EU created a stand-alone Committee of European Banking Supervisors (CEBS), which was independent from the ECB and appeared to cement the alternative approach in which supervisors were kept distinct from central banks, as had also long been the case in Belgium, Switzerland, Scandinavia and more recently in the UK with the establishment of the Financial Services Authority in late 2001. The Groupe de Contact was subsumed into CEBS, which was granted a permanent secretariat in London.

In effect, CEBS made the ECB's Banking Supervision Committee (with which it shared several members, namely those central banks that were banking supervisors) largely redundant, at least in terms of micro-prudential supervision. CEBS organised regular consultations among national banking supervisors and joint work on issues of common interest, but without either the authority or the means to

---

24 Notably, in the discussions that eventually led to the creation of BaFin, the Bundesbank argued it should be granted banking supervision authority in line with the ECB's recommendations at the time, but was overruled in the political decision-making process (Schüler, 2004, page 12).

enforce supervisory consistency. Meanwhile, the ECB's Banking Supervision Committee fostered attempts at crisis simulation and stress testing, but these initiatives encountered considerable pushback and were ultimately unable to generate a realistic shared analysis of the system's vulnerabilities[25].

Throughout that period, it was commonly reckoned that any policy integration in the area of financial services would happen first in the area of wholesale markets and securities regulation, rather than in banking, as the latter retained such close linkages with national governments and policies. This prioritisation was reflected, for example, in the European Commission's financial services action plan of 1999, a programme for the next years' legislative activity in that area (European Commission, 1999), and in the focus on securities markets oversight in a high-profile report from a committee chaired by central banker Alexandre Lamfalussy (Lamfalussy, 2001)[26].

Diagnoses of the shortcomings of the euro area's banking policy architecture continued to be made, but warnings failed to become a European policy consensus. In an in-depth analysis in 1998, the International Monetary Fund (IMF) criticised the lack of an explicit lender-of-last-resort role for the ECB and called for further policy integration: "*Through time, the introduction of the euro [...] may require the centralization of financial surveillance, systemic risk management,*

---

25   Two 'Eurosystem stress-testing exercises' were held in April 2005 and May 2006 respectively, and were followed by a conference in mid-July 2007, shortly before the inception of the great financial crisis (see https://www.ecb.europa.eu/pub/conferences/html/sfi_conf.it.html). They are described cursorily on pages 204-206 of the conference's published proceedings (ECB, 2008).

26   CEBS was itself modelled on the Committee of European Securities Regulators, created in 2001 as recommended by the Lamfalussy report. In the meantime, Lamfalussy had headed the European Monetary Institute, which had succeeded the Committee of Governors in January 1994 and gave way to the ECB in June 1998.

and crisis resolution. [...] the ECB will be at the center of European financial markets without the tools necessary for independently assessing creditworthiness of counterparties or the tools to provide direct support to solvent but illiquid institutions. This is not likely to be sustainable, and the ECB may soon be forced to assume a leading and coordinating role in crisis management and banking supervision" (IMF, 1998, pages 106 and 110).

In a noted speech delivered soon afterwards, Padoa-Schioppa dismissed the IMF's concerns about crisis management on the grounds that the ECB would be prepared to respond to emergency liquidity needs – a claim that was largely vindicated when crisis hit a decade later. He nevertheless concurred that it was *"absolutely necessary"* to move towards greater supervisory integration and *"allow a sort of euro area collective supervisor to emerge that can act as effectively as if there were a single supervisor."* Possibly out of diplomatic concerns, he simultaneously expressed scepticism that such integration must involve triggering the Maastricht Treaty's enabling clause: *"Although the Treaty has a provision that permits the assignment of supervisory tasks to the ECB, I personally do not rely on the assumption that this clause will be activated"* (Padoa-Schioppa, 1999).

Neither the IMF nor Padoa-Schioppa nor other analysts at the time, however, went as far as envisioning a scenario in which supervisory failures would be such that bank-solvency concerns would threaten the sovereign creditworthiness of one or several member state(s). Similarly, economist Paul De Grauwe, in an otherwise singularly lucid analysis of the risks of systemic financial instability in the soon-to-be-formed monetary union, did not explicitly envisage a scenario of sovereign credit stress, let alone euro-area breakup[27].

---

27 Paul De Grauwe, 'The euro and financial crises', *Financial Times*, 20 February 1998.

Investors likewise declined to price in the possibility of future sovereign credit problems, perhaps partly blindsided by the effective incentives for fiscal discipline during the 1990s among the countries that wanted to join the euro from its inception[28]. The sovereign debt spreads of all future euro-area countries (ie the difference between the market-determined interest rate of their long-term debt, eg with ten years' maturity, over the reference issuer, namely Germany) decreased to ultra-low levels during the late 1990s and remained there until 2008, a year into the great financial crisis. Most market participants and many policymakers had embraced the belief that a single market in financial services had emerged, in which financial conditions were equalised across all euro-area countries. The possibility of fragmentation of that financial system along national lines, through the increase in country spreads to significant levels, appeared implausible to most, despite the treaty-enshrined stipulations that euro-area countries could not mutualise their existing debt even in cases of financial turmoil.

Meanwhile, national authorities in Europe let the banks under their watch expand their balance sheets at a rapid pace from the mid-1990s, if not earlier (Bayoumi, 2017). As financial historian Harold James (2012b, page 393) summarised it:

"The first ten years of the Euro's existence were overshadowed by two long-running sagas, both of which attracted a great deal of public attention and seemed to define the struggle over the currency: struggles over the character of monetary policy and who made it,

---

28   Among the countries that initially decided to adopt the euro, only Greece had to face a delay, joining the monetary union two years late on 1 January 2001. Concerns about the durability of that fiscal discipline, however, became evident as early as 2003, when France and Germany jointly neutered the European Commission's efforts to implement the excessive deficit procedure established by the Maastricht Treaty.

and struggles over competitiveness. The debates deflected attention from the main issues, the unsustainability of Europe's (and the world's) approach to banking and the effects of the financialization explosion on public credit".

Only the actual and painful experience of crisis would reveal the risk nexus between banking systems and sovereign finance as the euro area's greatest practical vulnerability[29].

---

29 This view has become standard since the crisis. As one example among many, Charles Grant (2015) cited *"five serious design flaws"* in the initial design of the euro area, the second of which was *"that the plans for monetary union lacked provisions for a 'banking union,' which is now recognized as an essential component."*

3 DECISION POINT: THE EURO-AREA CRISIS AND THE BIRTH OF THE BANKING UNION PROJECT

On 30 July 2007, IKB Deutsche Industriebank, a mid-sized German bank, announced its rescue by public financial institution KfW, thus becoming the first banking casualty of what would soon become the great financial crisis[30]. The crisis escalated in subsequent months, including with the Northern Rock bank run in the United Kingdom in mid-September 2007, and hit full strength in September-October 2008 with a string of traumatic events occurring in rapid succession, the most acutely remembered being the Lehman Brothers bankruptcy on 15 September 2008.

From 2009-2010 events morphed into a crisis of the euro area. Other jurisdictions where turmoil had occurred in the first two years of crisis – the United States, the UK, Switzerland and Denmark – returned to financial stability. The euro-area crisis reached its climax in the period between summer 2011 and summer 2012, with dramatic but comparatively limited sequels in Cyprus in 2013 and Greece in 2015, and was essentially over by mid-2017. Only a few salient points are mentioned here as paving the way towards banking union, cherry-picking from a complex sequence of developments that several authors

---

30 'Great financial crisis' is preferred here to the alternative expression 'global financial crisis', because the financial disruption was concentrated in the North Atlantic region, even though the economic fallout was felt around the world.

have more comprehensively described and analysed (eg Bastasin, 2015; Bayoumi, 2017; Tooze, 2018; Rehn, 2020).

Supervisory failure and the bank-sovereign vicious circle

In most media narratives and public perceptions, the fiscal component was at the heart of the euro-area crisis, so that it is often referred to as the 'euro sovereign debt crisis'. The crisis also revealed structural weaknesses in several countries, not least Greece. To a great extent, however, the underlying story was one of banking sector fragility, at least as much as either budgetary incontinence or structural rigidities. Of the so-called crisis countries within the euro area, the fiscal element was unambiguously dominant only in Greece. In Ireland, Spain, Cyprus and Slovenia, the banking sector was the true epicentre of turmoil, with Portugal an intermediate case[31]. More importantly still, banking sector vulnerabilities in France, Germany and Italy influenced many of these larger countries' positions, and as a consequence, EU decisions as well.

Viewed from an EU standpoint, then, a central feature of the crisis was the colossal, near-universal failure of banking regulation and supervision. In principle, these two kinds of failure – regulatory and supervisory – are not necessarily correlated. One can imagine a lax regulatory setting being offset by rigorous supervision, because supervisors are usually empowered to impose more demanding requirements than the minimums set in banking regulations, in order to ensure that banks remain safe and sound, a capacity often referred to as

---

31   The role of banking sector fragility in the Portuguese crisis is detailed in Véron (2016), pages 22-27.

supervisory review or supervisory discretion[32]. Conversely, supervisory failures may occur even in the presence of adequate regulations if the latter are not properly enforced by supervisory authorities. Because strong supervision can partly compensate for lax regulations, whereas strong regulations cannot make up for deficient supervision, the focus here is generally on supervision more than on regulation. In practice, regulatory and supervisory failures are often correlated, especially when both result at least in part from an environment in which public authorities are prone to granting banks more generous treatment than the public interest would require.

In the runup to the crisis, all European banks were deemed by their national supervisors to be compliant with applicable capital requirements. But these requirements were too low, and the enforcement of compliance was too lax, with the result that most banks were severely undercapitalised by any reasonable economic yardstick. Of the 13 euro-area countries at the start of the crisis, only Finland did not experience any highly public case of blatant lapse of national prudential supervision, resulting in government-managed rescue at taxpayers' expense in the decade from 2007 to 2017[33]. This poor record

---

32 Supervisory discretion is embedded in the so-called Basel accords, which define the international framework for the prudential supervision of banks. These accords are named after the Basel Committee on Banking Supervision which sets them, itself hosted by the Bank for International Settlements in Basel, Switzerland. They distinguish between uniform 'pillar 1' minimum requirements resulting from the applicable regulations, and bank-specific 'pillar 2' requirements resulting from the supervisory review. An additional 'pillar 3' revolves around disclosure requirements meant to generate pressure from investors in the banks' shares (when listed) and bonds, known in the Basel parlance as market discipline.

33 There was no stand-alone case of egregious supervisory failure in Luxembourg, but that country was involved, together with Belgium, France and the Netherlands, in the high-profile collapses of Dexia and Fortis, as noted eg in the IMF's Financial System Stability Assessment in 2011 (IMF, 2011). Cyprus, Malta, Slovakia and the Baltic countries, having joined the euro area after the start of crisis, are excluded from this count, even though the observation of pervasive supervisory failure also applies at least to Cyprus and Latvia among these.

became blatantly visible early in the crisis sequence; a high-profile EU report published in February 2009 (and further discussed below) noted sternly that *"the evidence clearly shows that the crisis prevention function of supervisors in the EU has not been performed well, and is not fit for purpose"* (Larosière, 2009, page 42).

The European experience was also markedly different from that of the United States, where the most dramatic problems occurred in 'non-banks' under weaker supervisory regimes: consumer finance companies such as Household International, broker-dealers such as Bear Stearns and Lehman Brothers, thrifts such as IndyMac and Washington Mutual, insurers such as AIG, and government-sponsored enterprises such as Fannie Mae and Freddie Mac. US banking supervision was far from flawless but did not fail nearly as comprehensively as in Europe, even though the downward spiral of the crisis ultimately also threatened the viability of many US banks[34]. US authorities were also generally better prepared than their European peers to intervene in cases of bank failure[35].

In short, the euro area experienced a strikingly general failure of its bank supervisory regime based on near-exclusively national oversight. The most straightforward explanation is that the combination of market and monetary integration on the one hand, and preservation of near-

---

34   Citigroup has been cited widely as a case of a US supervisory lapse. Federal Reserve Chairman Ben Bernanke testified in 2009 that *"out of maybe the 13, 13 of the most important financial institutions in the United States, 12 were at risk of failure within a period of a week or two"* at the climax of crisis in September-October 2008 (Financial Crisis Inquiry Commission, 2011, page 354).

35   On three occasions, the US authorities triggered the legal mechanism known as systemic risk exception, allowing targeted support for fragile banks that might otherwise fail: for Wachovia on 29 September 2008, Citigroup on 23 November 2008, and Bank of America on 16 January 2009. Wachovia was subsequently purchased by Wells Fargo in a transaction that removed the need for public support. Citigroup and Bank of America both received an injection of preferred stock and benefitted from a public asset guarantee (FDIC, 2017, chapter 3).

exclusively national prudential supervision on the other hand, distorted the supervisors' incentives towards banking nationalism as opposed to their ostensible mandate of enforcing safety and soundness[36].

A vivid illustration of that drift was provided by the acquisition in 2007 of ABN AMRO, the Amsterdam-based international banking group, by a consortium that included Britain's Royal Bank of Scotland (RBS), the Benelux's Fortis and Spain's Santander, which soon profitably resold Banca Antonveneta, an Italian bank that ABN AMRO had just acquired in 2006, to Banca Monte dei Paschi di Siena. Particularly in the UK, Belgium and Italy, there was far too little scrutiny of the respective transactions, partly because the expansion of the local champions was viewed as intrinsically desirable. The legacy of the ABN AMRO acquisition played a significant role in the subsequent demise of all three acquirers: RBS and Fortis in 2008, and Monte dei Paschi gradually in later years. Conversely, national authorities in many instances acted to protect domestic banks against acquisition by foreign peers, leveraging their statutory authority to vet changes in shareholding control well beyond what would have been justified by prudential considerations[37].

Together with ineffective supervision, the other (and related) legacy with which Europe entered the great financial crisis was a high willingness of governments to use their own resources – taxpayers' money – to compensate for losses incurred by market participants in the wake of bank failures, or in colloquial terms, bail them out. To oversimplify a rather complex story, this 'deep-pocket' approach to bank crisis resolution became standard practice in Europe in the interwar

---

36 In some instances, 'nationalism' operated at the sub-national level, eg Spain's Autonomous Communities, Italy's provinces and communes, or Germany's *Länder*. See eg Otero-Iglesias *et al* (2016) on Spain, and Hellwig (2018) on Germany.

37 See for example Xavier Vives, 'European Banks Future on the Urge to Merge', *Wall Street Journal*, 13 May 2005, https://blog.iese.edu/xvives/files/2011/09/208.pdf.

period, with Austria's Creditanstalt, Germany's Danat-Bank, Dresdner Bank and Commerzbank, and Italy's three largest banks (Banca Commerciale Italiana, Credito Italiano and Banco di Roma), among the most internationally impactful cases. Thereafter, cases in which creditors of failing banks lost money, such as Bankhaus Herstatt in 1974 and Bank of Credit and Commerce International in 1991, were exceptions rather than the rule, and the fact that claimants lost money was typically viewed as a policy failure[38].

In Europe then, as in other parts of the world, including Canada and Japan, good crisis management practice was construed as boiling down to effective supervision so that no bank would fail (crisis prevention), or if a collapse was inevitable, early intervention to minimise the cost of the rescue to taxpayers and work out the troubled assets as efficiently as possible. Along these lines, the Swedish banking crisis of 1991-1992, in which the government reimbursed all creditors of failed banks, was generally counted as a policy success. Conversely, in cases of large-scale bailouts, such as Crédit Lyonnais in 1993, the public outcry was directed at the mismanagement of the bank and failure of public oversight, rather than at the principle of remedial use of taxpayers' money, which was viewed as inevitable once the losses had materialised.

Thus, in the early stages of the crisis starting in 2007, it was viewed as natural that a failing bank should be rescued by the government of its home country. In several instances, including IKB and RBS, even

---

38   The Herstatt crisis gave rise to several initiatives to create elements of a safety net and of risk reduction, including the establishment of deposit insurance (*Einlagesicherungsfonds*) and of a specialised institution to provide liquidity (*Liquiditäts-Konsortialbank*) by private-sector German banks, followed by that of the German savings banks' institutional protection scheme in 1975; the founding of the Basel Committee on Banking Supervision (Goodhart, 2011); and after much delay, the creation of the CLS System that started operating in 2002 to reduce risk in foreign-exchange transactions.

shareholders were compensated by the public purse to a significant extent; all creditors, including junior ones, were fully reimbursed in all these early cases. An extreme case was Ireland, where the government in late September 2008 formally guaranteed all bank deposits and almost all bank debt, on the premise that the banks were all solvent, which later turned out not to be true[39].

Like the supervisory forbearance, the 'deep-pocket' approach to bank crisis resolution was directly related to banking nationalism. Countries opting for harsher market discipline and losses to creditors of failing banks, the perception went, would see 'their' banks hamstrung by higher financing costs and possibly acquired by better-supported foreign rivals (Véron, 2013). Padoa-Schioppa, by then Italy's finance minister, called for a sector-wide review of bank soundness at the European level, implying triage of the weaker ones and restructuring of the hopeless cases. But this was decisively rejected by all other political leaders (Enria, 2020b)[40]. It was agreed instead, by broad consensus and at the particular insistence of Germany, that each country would take care of 'its' banks, including at the peak of financial-market dislocation in early October 2008 (Bastasin, 2015, chapters 1 and 2). As late as October 2011, the EU's official stance was that "*national governments should provide* [financial] *support*" to any bank that was not able to maintain a sound financial position by

---

39   Two years later, Ireland would also provide the first instance during the euro-area crisis in which subordinated bank creditors incurred losses, after the unsustainable guarantee had precipitated the entire country into an assistance programme.

40   See also Tommaso Padoa-Schioppa, 'Europe needs a single financial rule book', *Financial Times*, 10 December 2007, https://www.ft.com/content/b3c5f9c0-a750-11dc-a25a-0000779fd2ac.

market means[41].

As an increasing number of banks across Europe were revealed to be unsound, however, the national deep-pocket policy approach of bailing out all problem banks became increasingly unaffordable. As early as March 2008, as shown by later IMF research, *"a distinctively European banking crisis"* took shape in which *"sovereign spreads tended to rise with the growing demand for support by weakening domestic financial sectors, especially in countries with lower growth prospects and higher debt burdens"* (Mody and Sandri, 2011). In countries where banking systems were large relative to the broader economy because of high leverage and/or expansion abroad, that contingent liability threatened the very sustainability of public finances, to an extent that had not been anticipated in the formative period of monetary union, as covered in the previous chapter. In turn, incipient sovereign financial stress was naturally met by 'moral suasion' by public authorities on domestic banks so that they would facilitate sovereign financing, a form of financial repression that was later to be further enabled by the ECB's long-term refinancing operations in late 2011[42].

In autumn 2010, Ireland had to face austerity, and the humbling experience of an external assistance programme, because of the exorbitant

---

41 Euro Summit Statement of 26 October 2011, page 15, https://www.consilium.europa.eu/uedocs/cms_data/docs/pressdata/en/ec/125644.pdf. EU state-aid control mitigated some of the most distortionary impact of such financial assistance, but did not aim at averting it altogether.

42 French President Sarkozy memorably summarised the mechanism: *"This means that each state can turn to its banks, which will have liquidity at their disposal"* (cited by Paul Taylor, 'Exclusive - ECB limits bond buying, eurozone looks to banks', *Reuters*, 9 December 2011, https://www.reuters.com/article/uk-eurozone-ecb-exclusive-ecb-limits-bond-buying-eurozone-looks-to-banks-idUKTRE7B80OA20111209). On the resulting increase of domestic sovereign exposures, see James (2012a).

expense of rescuing its banks[43]. By summer 2011, these contagion dynamics were no longer limited to relatively small countries such as Greece, Ireland and Portugal[44]. Spain, Italy and France also experienced various forms of stress. In Spain, fragilities in the banking sector and especially the savings banks (*cajas de ahorros*) surfaced from late 2008, but their extent became more dramatically visible in late 2011, as a new government led by Mariano Rajoy was taking over (Baudino *et al*, 2023). The subsequent acceleration of the process of discovery led to the resignations, two weeks apart in late spring 2012, of the Bank of Spain's governor and deputy governor in charge of supervision (Véron, 2016, page 29). The corresponding contingent burden of bailing out the ailing banks' creditors made investors increasingly nervous about lending to the Spanish state. In Italy, the high level of government debt led to a parallel rise in bond spreads, brought about by concerns about sovereign creditworthiness, and in turn to a deterioration of financing conditions for the country's banks.

In France, during a few weeks in late August and early September 2011, investors started to question whether the state's historically strong guarantee of the country's large banks might become a source of vulnerability for the government's own financial signature. Consequently, the banks had difficulty accessing funding in US dollars and French sover-

---

43   This was not entirely unprecedented for an EU country, since the collapse of Parex Bank in 2008 had forced Latvia to seek assistance from the IMF. The context was markedly different, however, and the causality more multifaceted given Latvia's macroeconomic challenges. Economist Anders Aslund (2010, page 27) summarised: "*Although Latvia was also an accident waiting to happen, it could have held out for several months without an IMF program, if it had not been for Parex Bank.*"

44   Greece first received financial assistance from fellow euro-area member states and from the IMF in May 2010, followed by Ireland in November 2010 and Portugal in May 2011.

eign spreads started to rise as well[45]. While the market's focus on France turned out to be short-lived, the episode had a profound impact on bankers and policy officials in Paris, which would play a key role in their collective move away from banking nationalism in mid-2012, as detailed below. The disorderly dynamics are illustrated by Figure 1, which shows the spreads of the three countries' 10-year debts over Germany.

Figure 1: France, Italy, Spain, 10-year sovereign bond spread vs Germany (percentage points)

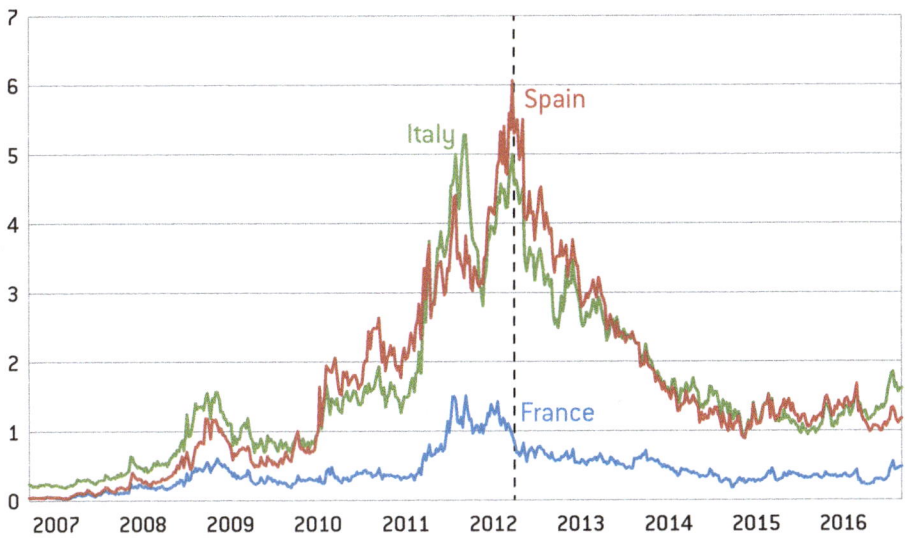

Source: Bloomberg.

In early 2009, informed by the observation of events particularly in Iceland and Ireland, IMF staff produced what appears to have been the

---

45   See Liz Alderman, 'Fears Rattle Big Banks in France', *New York Times*, 12 September 2011, https://www.nytimes.com/2011/09/13/business/global/turmoil-ensnares-big-french-banks.html.

first-ever diagnosis in the euro-area context of the vicious circle between overextended national banking sectors and sovereigns that insist on guaranteeing them (Mody, 2009). The bank-sovereign vicious circle narrative captured the core of the contagion mechanism that fuelled financial instability in the euro area, and became increasingly widely adopted by academics and other analysts during 2010 and 2011. By early 2012, its recognition as the engine of the euro-area crisis had become a matter of overwhelming consensus in policy circles.

In the second half of 2011, the increased awareness of the bank-sovereign vicious circle gave rise, logically, to proposals from within and outside policy institutions for fiscal policy integration, banking policy integration, or both. At a conceptual level, the IMF's chief economist, Olivier Blanchard, summarised the vicious circle in a crisp, graphical way in a series of presentations to policymakers during August and September 2011 (Véron, 2016, page 7). In November, the influential German Council of Economic Experts made the description of the bank-sovereign vicious circle a prominent feature of its widely commented annual report, together with a vigorous call for action by Germany to break it (GCEE, 2011; Schäfer, 2017, page 94). The high point of rhetorical advocacy of fiscal policy integration during that sequence was a speech by German Chancellor Angela Merkel at the Bundestag on 2 December 2011, in which she called for a *"fiscal union"* (*Fiskalunion*)[46]. Merkel made it clear, however, that her vision would not entail mutualisation of the member states' debts or joint issuance, but rather a straightjacket on national policies that would ensure fiscal prudence in all member states. As such, it could be viewed as a way to reduce sovereign credit risk over

---

46   Helen Pidd, 'Angela Merkel vows to create 'fiscal union' across eurozone', *The Guardian*, 2 December 2011, https://www.theguardian.com/business/2011/dec/02/angela-merkel-eurozone-fiscal-union.

the long-term, but in the short term was likely to exacerbate the vicious circle rather than mitigate or break it.

As for banking policy integration, a key development occurred in August 2011, when both the European Banking Authority (EBA)[47] and the IMF (Lagarde, 2011) started making public calls for direct recapitalisation of fragile European banks by a common euro-area fund, most likely the European Stability Mechanism (ESM), which was in the process of being established at the time. The ESM direct recapitalisation approach was promptly supported by the US government, which viewed it as functionally equivalent to its own 'stress tests' that had largely succeeded in restoring trust in the American banking system in the spring of 2009. At a mid-September 2011 meeting of European finance ministers in Wrocław, Poland, US Treasury Secretary Timothy Geithner advocated a forceful approach to cleaning up the euro-area banking sector. On 4 November, President Barack Obama similarly exhorted the leaders of France, Germany, Italy and Spain in a side session of the Group of Twenty summit meeting in Cannes (Bastasin, 2015, pages 328 and 334). In early December, European Council President Herman Van Rompuy, an economist by training who had worked at the National Bank of Belgium in the mid-1970s, in turn called in a public report to European leaders for *"introducing the possibility for the ESM to directly recapitalise banking institutions"* (Van Rompuy, 2011).

The expression 'banking union' was first introduced by the author into

---

47   *Market News International*, 'EBA Calls for Direct EFSF Bank Lending, More Capital – Press', 30 August 2011, https://www.forexlive.com/news/!/eba-calls-for-direct-efsf-bank-lending-more-capital-press-20110830. The EBA was established by EU legislation on 1 January 2011, as a somewhat reinforced version of the prior CEBS that had been created in 2004 (see chapter 2). It was led by Andrea Enria, who had worked with Padoa-Schioppa at the Bank of Italy, had been the secretary-general of the ECB's Banking Supervisory Committee from 1999 to 2004 and of CEBS from 2004 to 2008, and would later be head of ECB Banking Supervision from 2019 to 2023.

the public debate in December 2011, a fortnight after Merkel's Bundestag speech and with initial emphasis on the parallel between her fiscal union rhetoric and what needed to be done in banking policy (Véron, 2011; De Rynck, 2015, page 9)[48]. Its adoption became widespread following an article in the Financial Times in early April 2012, which used it in relation to a presentation during which ECB Executive Board member Jörg Asmussen advocated for the integration at European level of both prudential supervision and financial resources for crisis management. At the time, it was still unclear whether the banking union should be limited to the euro area, or would also include the UK and the entire EU single market[49]. The European Commission started referring to banking union in its public discourse in late May 2012[50]. Even after that, it took more than a year for EU countries to agree collectively on the use of the expression and the ambition it signalled[51].

In the meantime, a consensus had started to form in the EU policy community on what banking union should mean in practice. The ECB and IMF both played an important role in catalysing that consensus.

---

48 The author adopted the expression 'banking union' in preference to previous references to 'banking federalism' following a suggestion made to him by European Commission official Maarten Verwey, who had heard it on a recent occasion. The identity of the individual who coined the expression on that occasion remains as yet undetermined.

49 Alex Barker, 'Eurozone weighs union on bank regulation', *Financial Times*, 3 April 2012, https://www.ft.com/content/f03ab0bc-7d84-11e1-81a5-00144feab49a. As late as June 2012, observers envisaged a direct supervisory mandate being granted to the EBA, implying a geographical scope extending to the entire single market (Barker and Parker, 2012).

50 See James G. Neuger, 'EU Weighs Direct Aid to Banks as Antidote to Crisis', *Bloomberg*, 31 May 2012, https://www.bloomberg.com/news/articles/2012-05-30/eu-weighs-direct-aid-for-banks-common-bonds-as-crisis-antidote; and European Commission memo of 6 June 2012, 'The banking union', https://ec.europa.eu/commission/presscorner/detail/en/MEMO_12_413.

51 Reflecting on the matter, Van Rompuy (2014a) noted: "*I remember vividly only two years ago how careful we were not to employ the term 'banking union', out of a concern that this was politically too sensitive and people would go up the barricades.*"

The latter had been consistently ahead of the curve in previous years in making the case for European banking policy integration (eg Decressin *et al*, 2007; Fonteyne *et al*, 2010).

In November 2011, ECB Vice President Vitor Constâncio declared in a public speech: *"For the euro area I will say clearly: we need for cross-border banking institutions a European Resolution Authority, including or combined with a Resolution Fund, as well as a European Supervisor"* (Constâncio, 2011). The IMF's then Managing Director Christine Lagarde suggested a specific roadmap in January 2012: *"To break the feedback loop between sovereigns and banks, we need more risk sharing across borders in the banking system. In the near term, a pan-euro area facility that has the capacity to take direct stakes in banks* [ie ESM direct recapitalisation] *will help break this link. Looking further ahead, monetary union needs to be supported by financial integration in the form of unified supervision, a single bank resolution authority with a common backstop, and a single deposit insurance fund"* (Lagarde, 2012).

ECB President Mario Draghi in turn echoed this vision in April, albeit with less-precise wording: *"Ensuring a well-functioning EMU* [Economic and Monetary Union] *implies strengthening banking supervision and resolution at European level"* (Draghi, 2012). At the informal European Council meeting on 23 May 2012, country leaders asked Van Rompuy to produce a report within a few weeks on how to stop the rapid deterioration of financial conditions in the euro area. On that occasion, French President François Hollande, freshly elected earlier that month and prodded by Italian Prime Minister Mario Monti, spoke to journalists in favour of banking union, something his predecessor Nicolas Sarkozy had never done (Bastasin, 2015, page 374).

A fateful week in late June 2012

The policy momentum towards banking union, which built up gradually in the second half of 2011 and the first half of 2012, came suddenly to a point of decision during a sequence of three key meetings in late June of that year, coinciding with what a principal player has described as the most dangerous moment of the entire euro-area crisis (Rehn, 2020, page 172)[52].

On Friday 22 June in Rome, Mario Monti hosted Hollande, Merkel and Van Rompuy, in preparation for the European Council meeting scheduled for the following week; they were joined by Spain's Rajoy on his own initiative. During this gathering, the leaders did not get into technicalities but agreed that efforts should be accelerated to find a solution to the banking problems that fed the bank-sovereign vicious circle, and that to that end, their respective finance ministers should meet urgently and secretly. The ministers' meeting was scheduled to take place the next Tuesday evening at Charles De Gaulle (CDG) airport near Paris, an unusual choice of venue that combined the advantages of accessibility and discretion.

On Monday 25 June, Spain formally requested an assistance programme, including help from the soon-to-be established European Stability Mechanism, to address the mounting concerns about its banking sector. On Tuesday 26 June, in Brussels, Van Rompuy published the report leaders had asked him to prepare on 23 May. Since he had prepared it in coordination with his peers at the European Commission (José Manuel Barroso), Eurogroup (Jean-Claude Juncker)[53] and ECB (Mario Draghi), the text became known as the 'Four Presidents' Report'

---

52   In addition to the references in the text, the account provided here relies in part on the author's interviews of several key players involved in the policy sequence of late June 2012, who have opted not to be quoted individually.

53   The Eurogroup is formed by the finance ministers of euro-area countries.

(Van Rompuy, 2012)[54]. In it, Van Rompuy presented a blueprint for euro-area reform, providing an important reference point for subsequent discussions, with a combination of four interrelated efforts: banking union (*"an integrated financial framework* [that] *elevates responsibility for supervision to the European level, and provides for common mechanisms to resolve banks and guarantee customer deposits"*); fiscal union (*"an integrated budgetary framework* [that entails] *commensurate steps towards common debt issuance* [and] *different forms of fiscal solidarity"*); economic union (*"an integrated economic policy framework* [to] *promote sustainable growth, employment and competitiveness"*); and political union (*"ensuring the necessary democratic legitimacy and accountability of decision-making within the EMU, based on the joint exercise of sovereignty for common policies and solidarity"*). The placement of banking union in first position hinted at the fact that it would be the primary focus of action in the immediate near term[55].

Hours after the publication of Van Rompuy's report, the four countries' finance ministers and a few additional officials gathered as planned in a nondescript conference room at CDG airport's Sheraton hotel. They were ministers Wolfgang Schäuble for Germany, Pierre Moscovici for France, Vittorio Grilli for Italy and Luis de Guindos for Spain, senior ministry officials Thomas Steffen (Germany) and Ramon Fernandez (France), Hollande's deputy head of staff in

---

54   The name 'Four Presidents' Report' is also associated with a longer document on the same theme, which Van Rompuy produced in December 2012.
55   Partly in response to the growing banking sector distress in Spain and calls by various member states to supplement national banking supervision with a more reliable oversight mechanism, the ECB appears to have conducted an internal preliminary analysis in May-June 2012 of the feasibility of assuming a banking supervisory mandate on the basis of Article 127(6) TFUE (De Rynck, 2015, page 11). This analysis included a sketchy outline of how the corresponding tasks could be operationally separated from the conduct of monetary policy, as was later enshrined in the SSM Regulation.

charge of economic affairs, Emmanuel Macron, along with European Commissioner Olli Rehn, Van Rompuy's head of staff Frans van Daele, Euro Working Group chair Thomas Wieser, Commission Director-General for Economic Affairs Marco Buti, Rehn's adviser Taneli Lahti, and the head of the IMF's European Department, Reza Moghadam. During that meeting, the very existence of which remained secret until a press article revealed it eighteen months later[56], the essential political horse-trading was done that was later to define banking union – not without further twists or ironies.

Hollande, ostensibly prompted by Monti, had expressed support for banking union at the Brussels meeting on 23 May. This was new. The French government had consistently advocated direct recapitalisation of banks by the ESM, echoing the recommendations of the EBA and IMF in August 2011. The pooling at European level of prudential supervision, by contrast, had never previously received French support. Back in the early 1990s, as described in the previous chapter, the French Treasury had been among those opposing the insertion into the Maastricht Treaty of a supervisory role for the ECB. In early 2012, banking supervision was still viewed by most senior French officials (and bankers) as an instrument of national sovereignty that should be kept secure in Paris, even though the Treasury itself had started to consider alternative views, as detailed below. Several weeks after the May meeting, media still reported French banking supervisors, together with their Dutch and German peers, among "*very entrenched national authorities which have no intention of giving up power*" (Barker and Parker, 2012).

In that context, when Schäuble made an opening gambit at CDG as accepting the principle of ESM direct recapitalisation of Spanish

---

56   Peter Spiegel and Alex Barker, 'Banking union falls short of EU goal', *Financial Times*, 19 December 2013, https://www.ft.com/content/f1c23942-68cd-11e3-bb3e-00144feabdc0.

banks – the immediate focus of concern at the time – on condition of genuine European banking supervision, it was both a breakthrough and a hardball stance. It was a breakthrough, because Germany had until then rejected outright any ESM direct recapitalisation. At the same time, Schäuble was playing hardball, because he had good reason to believe that his condition would not be acceptable to his French counterparts, and that European-level prudential supervision would be viewed as a German demand that needed resisting[57]. In fact, views in Germany on European banking supervisory integration were far from unanimous. There were longstanding supporters, including commercial banks led by Deutsche Bank, which had advocated it for many years. By contrast, the influential public and cooperative banks were hostile to any pooling of banking policy at European level. They feared it would inevitably lead to less favourable treatment of their idiosyncratic arrangements. The Bundesbank had long been hostile to an ECB role in the supervision of individual banks, on the basis that it would harm the integrity of monetary policy[58], and continued to argue that it would be dangerous to

---

57 Schäfer (2017) noted that Hollande, in his remarks following the informal European Council in May 2012, had spoken firmly in favour of supervisory integration (page 117): "*I myself said that I want financial supervision mechanisms, deposit guarantees and crisis resolution to be integrated. [...] The more you coordinate and centralize, the better the response is on supervision, crisis resolution and above all deposit guarantees.*" But based on his interviews, Schäfer also indicated the opinion among French officials at the time of the CDG meeting that Schäuble's joint supervisor proposal "*was put as a condition we would never accept*" (page 121).

58 According to a close witness, "*Germany had strongly resisted it [pooled banking supervision] even when the financial crisis was at its peak, in 2009*" (van Middelaar, 2019, page 56). In an interview, Lamfalussy recalled that during the early phases of the great financial crisis, the ECB had no knowledge of the true situation of the euro area's banking sector "*because the Germans opposed it. They thought that by going into that new task* [of banking sector oversight even if only at the macroprudential level], *the ECB risked perverting its basic mandate that is to monitor the currency*" (Lamfalussy, 2013, page 173; author's translation).

embark on banking union without simultaneous fiscal union[59].

Unexpectedly, however, Macron, speaking on behalf of Hollande, accepted the *quid pro quo* instantly and directed the discussion towards how to implement in practice Schäuble's integrated supervision idea. For reasons of expediency, he advocated using the Maastricht Treaty's enabling clause as the legal basis for European supervision, which had also been recommended earlier in the day in Van Rompuy's Four Presidents' report[60].

Meanwhile, all participants made a conscious decision to not put deposit insurance on the agenda, even though it had been explicitly mentioned in Van Rompuy's report[61]. This choice was also motivated by expediency, because they were aware of the political sensitivity of deposit insurance particularly in Germany, and because of the perceived greater urgency of direct recapitalisation of Spanish banks by the ESM[62].

The sudden and unreserved French acceptance of European banking supervision must be understood in the context of a fast-changing

---

59 James Wilson, 'Bundesbank warns on EU banking union', *Financial Times*, 12 June 2012, https://www.ft.com/content/79c17794-b467-11e1-bb68-00144feabdc0.

60 Van Rompuy (2012), page 4. The triggering of the enabling clause of Article 127(6) TFEU was not technically without precedent, since it had already been used as basis for a regulation adopted in 2010 (Regulation (EU) 1096/2010) to enable the ECB to support the newly established European Systemic Risk Board. That text, however, was incomparably less impactful and contentious than the establishment of integrated European banking supervision. Schäfer (2017, page 121) corroborates the view that the *"main discussions* [at CDG] *took place between Schäuble and Macron"*.

61 Throughout this text, the expressions 'deposit insurance' and 'deposit guarantee' are used as synonyms. EU legislation refers to national arrangements as deposit guarantee schemes, whereas 'deposit insurance' is generally used when similar arrangements are considered at the European level.

62 Ironically enough, a subset of EU countries including France and Germany had formally endorsed the principle of European deposit insurance just a few days earlier in the Group of Twenty (G20) leaders' declaration at Los Cabos, Mexico, on 19 June 2012: *"Euro Area members of the G20 will take all necessary measures to safeguard the integrity and stability of the area, improve the functioning of financial markets and break the feedback loop between*

environment in France. The market turmoil episode in August-September 2011 had shattered long-held certainties in Paris about the optimality of the French bank-state nexus, in which the state would rescue any failing bank (as it had done with Crédit Lyonnais) and the banks would accept state guidance for their lending on matters of national interest. Within the French Treasury, there were animated debates in early 2012 between those who defended the traditional symbiosis with the national banking community and those who felt that defending the credit of the French state might require putting some newfound distance between it and the banks. The head of the Treasury at the time, Ramon Fernandez, was convinced of the need for ESM direct recapitalisation, and willing to accept changes to the traditional French stance on supervisory sovereignty to secure it. The election cycle just a few weeks earlier, with the presidential election won by Hollande in early May 2012 and parliamentary elections won by his centre-left party in June, had brought in a new political team whose principal members had comparatively little baggage on banking policy, having been absent from the multiple crisis management episodes of the previous five years[63].

The breakthrough at CDG airport set the stage for the next and more public major step, the European Council meeting and euro-area summit on 28-29 June in Brussels. Whereas much of the reporting of that meeting

---

sovereigns and banks. [...] Towards that end, we support the intention to consider concrete steps towards a more integrated financial architecture, encompassing banking supervision, resolution and recapitalization, and deposit insurance." The German authorities never subsequently appeared to feel bound by that pledge, however.

[63] De Rynck (2017, page 129) referred to France's acceptance of European banking supervision in 2017 as a *"U-turn compared to its 2010 preference of keeping supervision national."* Van Middelaar (2019, page 55) suggested that the transition from Sarkozy to Hollande allowed Van Rompuy to foster a *"No taboos"* mindset when putting the structural challenges of euro-area financial architecture onto the agenda of the 23 May summit. It may be noted, however, that banking sector policy was not a theme of partisan divide during the spring's election campaigns.

has centred on a combative move by Monti to impose his vision of European support for Italian sovereign debt via ESM bond purchases, that episode turned out to be considerably less consequential than the dynamics of decision-making about banking union that happened in parallel (and which Monti also supported). At the same time as the heads of state and government were meeting in Brussels's Justus Lipsius building on the evening of Thursday 28 June, their advisers ('sherpas') and senior finance ministry officials gathered in another room in the same building, where they worked on several successive drafts on the combination of European banking supervision and ESM direct bank recapitalisation that the participants in the CDG meeting had agreed two days earlier.

The critical issue was the sequential articulation between the two components of the *quid pro quo*. Creating a viable system of European banking supervision, based on Article 127(6) TFEU and consequently centred on the ECB, was acknowledged to be a medium-term effort, requiring at least several months of legislative process and perhaps a year for subsequent operational preparation. In the heated crisis conditions of the moment, that felt like a very long time, with multiple procedural uncertainties along the way and no guarantee of eventual effectiveness.

Conversely, the direct recapitalisation by the ESM of banks in need would be full of pitfalls, but if executed well, could be achieved comparatively very quickly, and the signal of risk pooling was felt by most of the measure's advocates to be needed as a matter of immediate urgency[64]. An initial draft, prepared by the Eurogroup Working Group

---

64   The precise structure of direct recapitalisation transactions was never made publicly explicit, even though it is likely to have been detailed in drafts shared among the negotiators. An official from the ESM described it much later as *"putting a large equity investment into the viable part of a bankrupt systemic bank"* (ESM, 2019, page 294).

secretariat led by Wieser together with the European Commission, attempted to square that circle by referring to ESM direct recapitalisation taking place after the ECB-centred supervisory mechanism has been established, but adding the sentence: *"Interim solutions will be set up for the direct recapitalisation of* [credit] *institutions by the ESM for the time during which this mechanism is being set up."*

The sherpas' meeting concluded around midnight with a revised version of the draft declaration that included a slightly amended version of that sentence, preserving the concept of *"interim solutions."* But that was opposed in the early hours of Friday 29 June by three of the assembled political leaders: Finland's Jyrki Katainen, the Netherlands' Mark Rutte and Merkel. Draghi did not defend the *"interim solutions"* but rather hinted at the possibility of retroactive application by which the ESM, in the medium-term future after the start of European banking supervision, would take over the capital instruments that would have been initially provided by individual countries, thus eventually assuming the corresponding risk on a pooled basis. For Draghi, the critical benefit of the package appears to have been the strong affirmation of the leaders' trust in the ECB, expressed by granting it supervisory authority over banks, which he presumably assessed as more important than the immediate risk-pooling through the ESM[65]. Merkel also strongly supported the single supervisory concept during the meeting, and insisted on adding an end-2012 deadline for its legislative elaboration (van Middelaar, 2019, page 57).

The final declaration, adopted amid general fatigue at 4:35 am on 29 June (Rehn, 2020, page 188) and published immediately afterwards,

---

65 An additional consideration for the ECB was that its greatly expanded and longer-term extension of liquidity to banks, through the long-term refinancing operations that Draghi had announced in late 2011, exposed it to unsustainable risk unless it gained more insight on the financial conditions of the recipient entities (De Rynck, 2015, page 11).

kept the reference to ESM direct recapitalisation but with no mention left of any *"interim solutions."* Following the multiple rounds of drafting, the key text was convoluted: *"The Commission will present Proposals on the basis of Article 127(6) for a single supervisory mechanism shortly. We ask the Council to consider these Proposals as a matter of urgency by the end of 2012. When an effective single supervisory mechanism is established, involving the ECB, for banks in the euro area the ESM could, following a regular decision, have the possibility to recapitalize banks directly."* This tortured language, however, was preceded by an unusually straightforward and forceful statement of purpose: *"We affirm that it is imperative to break the vicious circle between banks and sovereigns"*[66].

In sum, the late-June summit provided a strong basis for future ECB banking supervision, albeit with numerous risks and uncertainties about its eventual implementation. On crisis management, it endorsed the principle of ESM direct recapitalisation but kicked its implementation into the long grass. It made no commitment whatsoever on common deposit insurance.

The main departure from the policy balance that the participants in the CDG meeting had outlined was about ESM direct recapitalisation. It is difficult to disentangle the causes of that difference from the complex relationship between Merkel and Schäuble, which may have involved different approaches to policy and crisis management, as well as a longstanding political rivalry. It is also hard to disentangle the causes from the German coalition dynamics of the time, which included a partner (the Free Democratic Party) that was even more reticent than Schäuble on euro-area-wide risk-sharing. On the face of it, Merkel's preference appears to have been complete rejection of ESM direct

---

66 Euro Area Summit Statement of 29 June 2012, https://www.consilium.europa.eu/media/21400/20120629-euro-area-summit-statement-en.pdf.

recapitalisation, in line with the prior German stance[67], while Schäuble felt bound by his commitment at CDG. The language of the 29 June declaration, without the reference to interim solutions, was somewhere between these two positions, leaving neither of the two Germans fully satisfied. As will be detailed below, Merkel's restrictive vision on ESM use eventually prevailed through the subsequent developments, but that was partly offset by the creation of a single resolution mechanism that embedded a degree of risk-sharing that in turn might be eventually 'backstopped' by the ESM. The other side of the bargain, on pooling banking supervisory authority, turned out to be extremely resilient.

Banking union and crisis resolution

The weeks that followed the 29 June declaration were chaotic but decisive. At some point in early July, Merkel appears to have made a firm determination that a Greek exit from the euro area was too risky to be attempted. Meanwhile, in negotiations on the implementation of the decisions made in late June, German officials further backtracked on the commitment to use the ESM for direct bank recapitalisations in Spain, even in the somewhat distant future. Part of the motivation for their unusual behaviour[68] may have been linked to concerns that it could undermine the case they were making at the same time before the German Constitutional Court that the ESM was compatible with Germany's fundamental law. The court held a tense hearing on 10

---

67   The less obstructive version of that stance, as also formulated by the Bundesbank in June 2012, was to link banking union to a condition of simultaneous fiscal union. Barker and Parker (2012) thus wrote on 18 June 2012: *"Before exposing German taxpayers to foreign liabilities – such as deposit insurance or direct stakes in banks – Angela Merkel, German chancellor, wants federal controls over national banks and a fiscal union. In other words, some shared control of national tax and spending."*

68   In EU practice, decisions of leaders' summits such as that of 28-29 June 2012 are generally respected as binding all parties.

July in Karlsruhe before eventually approving the ESM construct in September, albeit with qualifications (ESM, 2019, chapter 26). As news filtered about the German backpedalling, markets became increasingly jittery[69]. Eventually, on 26 July, in front of an audience of financial market participants in London, Draghi uttered the memorable words *"within our mandate, the ECB is ready to do whatever it takes to preserve the euro – and believe me, it will be enough"*[70]. As Figure 1 illustrates, this marked a major turning point, after which the market crisis de-escalated rapidly, even before the ECB formally followed up on Draghi's words by announcing its programme of Outright Monetary Transactions on 6 September.

In several subsequent speeches, Draghi hinted at a causal link between the political leaders' show of support for the ECB on 29 June and his landmark assertion of purpose in London (eg Draghi, 2013). He never made that link fully explicit, however, as that would imply a dent in the ECB's sacrosanct principle of independence of monetary policy from any political considerations. Van Rompuy could afford to be more direct, at least after some time had passed. He dedicated a speech to this matter at the ECB in Frankfurt two years later, a fortnight after the effective start of its prudential supervisory mandate on 4 November 2014, and a fortnight before the end of his own term as European Council President. In his address, Van Rompuy highlighted the significance of the late-June summit, of which he described the key dynamics:

> *"The banking union is the biggest leap forward since the creation of the euro. [...] The June 2012 summit was perhaps the most*

---

69 See for example Joshua Chaffin, 'Euro doubts fuel leap in bond yields', *Financial Times*, 6 July 2012, https://www.ft.com/content/aab7d784-c787-11e1-85fc-00144feab49a.

70 See European Central Bank, 'Verbatim of the remarks made by Mario Draghi', 26 July 2012, https://www.ecb.europa.eu/press/key/date/2012/html/sp120726.en.html.

important European Council of my five years in office. [...] Leaders sensed that the moment called for a qualitative breakthrough. They also realised it had to be on banking union, the most urgent issue of all. [...] Some wanted to start with banking supervision, to prevent new problems, others preferred action on greater solidarity in the area of banking, to overcome troubles from the past. [...] We tied two political decisions together: the creation of a single supervisory mechanism for all eurozone banks and the possibility for failing banks to get capital directly from a common rescue fund" (ie the ESM).

Van Rompuy went further than Draghi ever would in public:

"*I will never forget, a couple of hours later on that Friday, Mario Draghi walking into my office [...] A man under huge pressure, for the first time in the eight months during which I'd seen him at work, he now looked relieved. 'Herman,' he said, 'Do you realise what you all did last night? This is the game-changer we need.' The commitment of political leaders to European banking supervision created the opening he needed for his own institution to step up its role in the crisis – with words, now famous words* [in London on 26 July], *and with action, the OMT* [Outright Monetary Transactions], *which both came that summer. It was a turning point.*"

Van Rompuy added pointedly: "*For a Central Bank, being independent does not mean being disconnected. That's why the ECB presidents attend meetings of the European Council, the Euro Summits, the Eurogroup and of the European Parliament*" (Van Rompuy, 2014b)[71].

That reading has been corroborated by other key participants in the events. Former ECB Executive Board member Peter Praet commented in a 2019 interview: "*The market panic of 2012 could only be stopped by Mario Draghi. Of course, the background for the success of his 'whatever it takes' line was the June European Council meeting of heads of state and governments, about putting in place the banking union and crisis management mechanisms. So that was the political background*"[72]. Several French participants have similarly described a direct link between the euro-area summit and the ECB's action[73]. Other participants still deny that such a link existed. Of course, whether the ECB would have intervened as it did, had the prior decision to establish European banking supervision not been taken, is ultimately impossible to establish

---

71   Van Rompuy's line that the ECB should be "*independent but not disconnected*" may have been a discreet tribute to the late Padoa-Schioppa, who often emphasised that the ECB's "*independence should not mean institutional loneliness*" (eg Bini Smaghi, 2011).

72   Rebecca Christie, 'Convincing the markets: Peter Praet revisits the ECB's unconventional monetary policy response to the euro crisis', *Finance & Development*, September 2019, https://www.imf.org/en/Publications/fandd/issues/2019/09/peter-praet-on-ECB-and-euro-crisis-trenches.

73   In an interview in late 2022, former French Treasury head Ramon Fernandez reminisced: "*During all these years, there was a kind of quid pro quo between governments and the ECB. Governments needed to see the ECB playing its part, and the ECB could not act without a very strong action from governments. [...] The ECB is totally independent, but the ECB could act when governments were acting. And in major cases, this is exactly what happened. For example, in 2012, when governments go into the banking union, the ECB / Mario Draghi is able to have his speech about 'whatever it takes' in late July.*" See Tim Gwynn Jones, 'In the Room' podcast, December 2022, https://uk-podcasts.co.uk/podcast/in-the-room-1/ramon-fernandez. Hollande succinctly gave the same narrative in his memoirs of the period: "*That night [28-29 June], our commitment to the French-German couple saved the single currency, overcame market speculators, and above all gave the ECB President space for more accommodative policy. A month later, in the midst of summer on 26 July 2012, Mario Draghi stated that he 'would do whatever it takes to preserve the euro'. Angela Merkel and I decided to publish a joint communiqué the next day. That day marked the beginning of the end of the euro area crisis. The European summit of 28 June 2012 was historic. Has this been sufficiently observed?*" (Hollande, 2018, chapter 6; author's translation).

with complete certainty.

By early September, many market participants had already concluded that the existential phase of the euro-area crisis was over. Ironically, this in turn reduced some of the pressure on policymakers to achieve what they had committed to, and facilitated the eventual neutering of the 29 June decision on ESM direct recapitalisation. Meanwhile, the leaders' decision on ECB banking supervision was implemented faithfully.

How euro-area leaders were able to achieve such a radical decision has been tentatively analysed by several authors (eg Epstein and Rhodes, 2014; De Rynck, 2015; Glöckler, Lindner and Salines, 2017; Schäfer, 2017; Nielsen and Smeets, 2018). Five key elements emerge from the account presented here.

- First, the existing system based on national banking supervision had failed so comprehensively that it could not be defended.
- Second, the imperative of averting a breakup of the euro area, which was reasonably viewed as an unacceptable option by everyone involved, concentrated the minds of policymakers and forced them to set stark priorities. It is striking that, at the moment of decision, longstanding policy positions of the respective national banking sectors appear to have been far less powerfully influential in the calculations of the political principals than in ordinary times.
- Third, the central role of the bank-sovereign vicious circle in driving contagion and dislocation was accepted as a matter of fact, and that provided a strong basis for consensus on policy choices.
- Fourth, there was a serendipitous alignment of circumstances, with both opportunity and urgency from the combination of, among other events, the electoral cycles in France and Greece (with a sense of fragile respite in the latter, following two successive parliamentary elections on 6 May and 17 June), and the perception of fast-escalating

crisis in the Spanish banking sector.
- Fifth, several individuals displayed outstanding leadership qualities: EU officials who pushed for decisions and national politicians who accepted painful compromises. France and Germany both made significant concessions, as did other member states in their wake. France renounced the principle of national sovereignty over banking supervision. Germany eventually backtracked on ESM direct recapitalisation, but it crucially accepted that all its banks – including the restive public and cooperative banks, on which more in the next chapter – would be covered by the new supervisory mechanism.

As Nielsen and Smeets (2018, page 1251) put it, *"there was nothing inevitable about the banking union."* It took much statesmanship to see, in the heat of the intense bargaining, that the agreement forged in the early hours of 29 June 2012 was net positive for every country involved.

4 EUROPEAN BANKING SUPERVISION: AN OLD DREAM COME TRUE

This chapter focuses on European banking supervision, also known as the Single Supervisory Mechanism (SSM) in the somewhat euphemistic language of the euro-area summit statement of 29 June 2012: the new architecture of bank prudential supervision in the euro area, centred on the ECB in Frankfurt, enacted in EU law through a Regulation of 15 October 2013 (the SSM Regulation)[74], and in force since 4 November 2014[75].

European banking supervision, thus defined, fulfils a vision that, as recounted in chapter 2, had been articulated in the European financial policy community since the 1960s, but was long considered too ambitious to be implemented or even merely mentioned in public. What was for a long time no more than a dream has become an established reality. Furthermore, as will be argued below, European

---

74 Council Regulation (EU) 1024/2013 of 15 October 2013.
75 Following ECB practice, the ECB together with the national supervisors, in their prudential supervisory capacity as defined by the SSM Regulation, are collectively referred to here as 'European banking supervision,' whereas the ECB's own supervisory arm within that collective is referred to as 'ECB banking supervision.' These semantic choices are preferred to reference to the SSM, which depending on context may mean either European banking supervision or ECB banking supervision and can therefore be confusing (market participants often refer to 'the ECB SSM' meaning ECB banking supervision). The SSM acronym is retained with reference to the SSM Regulation.

banking supervision has been effective so far, with a tangible impact in terms of the safety and soundness of euro-area banks.

Legislation

As was called for in the summit statement, the European Commission – specifically, its directorate-general for internal market matters including financial services, under Commissioner Michel Barnier – spent the summer of 2012 preparing a draft of the SSM legislation that would establish the integrated supervisory concept that was first agreed at CDG airport on 26 June. The ECB took an active role in supporting the Commission's legislative drafting work, to an extent that has been described as the two institutions *"jointly drafting"* the proposal (Nielsen and Smeets, 2018, page 1241). Barnier made the text public on 12 September 2012[76].

The European Commission's proposal set out a highly centralised concept for prudential supervision of banks in the euro area. It stipulated that the ECB would be the sole authority to grant or withdraw banking licenses – in contrast to the United States, where banks are chartered either at state or federal level[77]. The ECB would exercise its authority over all banks no matter how small, with the possibility to outsource supervisory tasks to the pre-existing national banking supervisors (referred to as *"national competent authorities"*), but retaining all decision-making powers on prudential matters, including on monitoring and enforcing compliance with capital, leverage and liquidity requirements.

---

76 The EU treaties grant the European Commission an exclusive role in making legislative proposals, which are then debated by the European Parliament and the EU Council ('co-legislators') under procedures that vary depending on which treaty article forms the basis for the policy – in this case Article 127(6), which requires unanimity in the EU Council and gives only a consultative role to the Parliament.
77 In the US context, 'national' banks are those chartered at the federal level, while the others are known as state banks.

The specific language of the European treaties constrained what the Commission could propose, since everyone agreed that any process of treaty change, no matter how minor, would be too lengthy and risky to be considered. Because Article 127(6) TFEU, the 'enabling clause' adopted at Maastricht that provided the treaty basis for the proposal, refers to "*specific tasks concerning policies relating to the prudential supervision of credit institutions*", the ECB would not be empowered on matters other than prudential issues, such as consumer protection or anti-money-laundering (AML) supervision. The proposal also did not attempt to modify the governance of the ECB as set in the treaty, under which all policy decisions must be made by the Governing Council. To accommodate this constraint, the proposal created a new intermediate body within the institution, the ECB Supervisory Board, which would prepare decisions but not formally take them, even though the no-objection procedure set out in the legislation means that the ECB Supervisory Board is where the decisions are made for most practical purposes[78].

Article 127(6) TFEU also combined with the balance between euro-area and non-euro-area countries within the EU to shape the process of legislative discussion. It required unanimous EU Council approval, with only a consultative role for the European Parliament. The UK, outside of the euro area, had decided not to obstruct the euro area's efforts towards common crisis resolution (Rogers, 2017), but still sought to extract something in exchange for its approval of the SSM Regulation, in the form of a revision of the governance of the EBA so that the British member of the EBA's decision-making Board of Supervisors would not

---

78 The draft decisions prepared by the ECB Supervisory Board are considered adopted unless the Governing Council objects within ten working days, or 48 hours in cases of emergency (Teixeira, 2020, page 227).

be systematically outvoted by euro-area members acting jointly. That implied that two separate legislative texts, the SSM Regulation and a revision of the EBA Regulation of 2010, would be negotiated and adopted in parallel. Since the EBA Regulation's revision was subject to the EU's ordinary legislative procedure, which requires the assent of both the European Parliament and the EU Council, the UK's stance effectively gave the European Parliament a veto over the SSM Regulation as well. That meant a more complex legislative process for the eventual adoption of the SSM Regulation, but also arguably greater democratic legitimacy once adopted than implied by the letter of Article 127(6).

With these legislative dynamics in mind, the initial discussion between EU countries in autumn 2012 led to the European Commission's proposal being amended on one important aspect, namely a reduction of the scope of direct ECB supervisory authority over smaller banks, dubbed "less significant institutions" in the revised text. This was a politically important point for Germany, where two nationwide networks of small banks wield considerable political influence, grouped through mutual support arrangements known in EU law as institutional protection schemes (IPSs)[79]: the Savings Banks Group (*Sparkassen-Finanzgruppe*) of public banks at local and regional levels of government (respectively, *Sparkassen* and *Landesbanken*); and the Cooperative Financial Group, member banks of which are owned by their retail customers (*Genossenschaftliche FinanzGruppe Volksbanken Raiffeisenbanken*). After some back-and-forth, it was agreed in the autumn of 2012 that the threshold generally separating 'significant' from 'less-significant' institutions would be set at €30 billion, implying

---

79   IPSs were only codified in EU law in the Capital Requirements Regulation of 2013, but the corresponding mutual support arrangements have been formally or informally in place for longer, going back to the 1930s for cooperative banks and to the mid-1970s for the public banks.

that twelve entities within the two German IPSs would be designated as significant and thus put under direct ECB supervision[80].

The introduction of the significant/less-significant distinction did not fundamentally alter the nature of the proposal, however. In fact, the ECB appeared to welcome it, since it would lighten the operational difficulty of the transition to European supervision and would allow ECB staff to focus on the larger potential problem banks[81]. Even with the amendments, the ECB was to retain ultimate authority over the smaller institutions' banking licenses, and on other key decisions such as authorising any change of controlling shareholder. Furthermore, the smaller banks in aggregate only represent about 17 percent of total euro-area banking assets, of which close to half (in terms of aggregate assets) is held in the two German IPSs (Lehmann and Véron, 2021). With respect to these German IPSs, as well as similar arrangements in Austria, the ECB was to retain leverage through its direct supervision of the largest

---

80   These significant institutions include, for the Savings Banks Group, a national financial services entity (DekaBank), the five main *Landesbanken* (BayernLB, Helaba, HSH Nordbank, LBBW, and Nord/LB), the former *Landesbank* in Berlin and the largest of the Sparkassen (Hamburger Sparkasse); and for the Cooperative Financial Group, the two central entities (DZ Bank and WGZ Bank, which later merged) and the two largest cooperative institutions (Deutsche Apotheker- und Ärztebank, and Münchener Hypothekenbank). HSH Nordbank later left the Savings Banks IPS as it was converted into a joint-stock company, acquired by private equity investors, and renamed Hamburg Commercial Bank in 2019. Twelve more banks in the two German IPSs, with €239 billion in aggregate assets as of end-2021, are designated as high-impact less-significant institutions under closer watch by the ECB (see below and ECB, 2023).

81   In its November 2012 opinion on the European Commission's proposal for the SSM Regulation, the ECB stated that the legislation *"should specify that the ECB should have recourse to national competent authorities for the performance of supervisory tasks, in particular regarding credit institutions of lesser economic, financial or prudential relevance, without prejudice to the ECB's right to provide guidance and instructions, or assume the tasks of national authorities when duly required"* (ECB, 2013).

entities[82]. As mentioned above, the fact that the ECB was granted such authority was a significant concession by Germany, in contrast to its longstanding stance of preserving the distinctiveness of its public and cooperative banking groups. While negotiating the SSM Regulation in the second half of 2012, the German authorities did relay the two IPSs' combative lobbying to secure a full exemption from ECB oversight, but at no point made it a deal-breaker[83], and in the end accepted a compromise that implied ECB authority over the IPSs, even though that authority was mostly indirect. The amendments, including the distinction between

---

82 Austria also has two IPSs, as in Germany respectively of savings banks (*Sparkassengruppe Österreich*) and cooperative banks (*Raiffeisen Bankengruppe*). There are differences with Germany, however. The Austrian savings banks, unlike their German peers, are private-sector entities, and their Sparkassengruppe is entirely under the ECB's direct supervisory authority as a single group, similarly to decentralised cooperative banking groups in other countries including Finland, France and Italy. The Raiffeisen Banking Group is broadly similar in structure to the German Cooperative Financial Group, with two of the entities of the IPS, Raiffeisen Bank International and Raiffeisenlandesbank Oberösterreich, designated as significant institutions (as of 2024) and thus under direct ECB supervision. Smaller IPSs also exist in Italy and Spain, and outside of the euro area in Poland.

83 See for example *Deutschlandfunk*, interview with Schäuble, 3 September 2012, https://www.wolfgang-schaeuble.de/der-bundesfinanzminister-im-dlf-interview-zur-europaeischen-bankenaufsicht/; Michael Steen, 'One regulator for all banks, says Draghi', *Financial Times*, 6 December 2012, https://www.ft.com/content/3a3730b4-3fd1-11e2-9f71-00144feabdc0. The comment by Martin Hellwig (2014, page 13) that *"Germany, it seems, was pushing* [in late June 2012] *for European control as a prerequisite to making ESM funds available to Spanish banks, perhaps without appreciating that this might also involve European control over German banks,"* might be viewed as overly dismissive in this context. Schäfer (2017, page 154) indicated, based on his interviews with French and German officials, that the initial German position following the publication of the European Commission's legislative proposal in September 2012 was to set the significance thresholds at €100 billion in total assets, and that in subsequent negotiating rounds this was lowered to €50 billion but with *Sparkassen* and *Landesbanken* specifically excluded. By contrast, the French initial proposal was a threshold at €5 billion. The final compromise at €30 billion (including all *Sparkassen* and *Landesbanken* above that level) can be viewed as demonstrating the negotiators' eagerness to find a compromise solution. Significantly, it is permanently set at that level and not inflation adjusted. As a consequence and all things equal, unless there is a revision of the SSM Regulation, the number of banks determined as significant is bound to slowly increase.

significant and less-significant institutions, were adopted by the EU Council in mid-December 2012.

The SSM Regulation went through further delays at the European Parliament which secured, among other changes, an agreement with the ECB on information sharing (De Rynck, 2015, page 6)[84], and a greater role than in the initial proposal in the process of appointing key ECB supervisory officials. More delays came with the approach of the German general election of 22 September 2013, out of fears that publishing the regulation before that date might generate a domestic political backlash in Germany. The SSM Regulation was finally enacted three weeks after the German election, on 15 October 2013. Altogether it was not very different from what the European Commission had proposed more than a year earlier. The longer-than-expected legislative process resulted in the date of transfer of supervisory authority to the ECB over the larger banks being set in the final text at 4 November 2014, instead of 1 July 2013 in the Commission's initial proposal. That delay, however, brought some benefits, since it gave the ECB more time to prepare the massive task of ensuring a smooth transition, including the comprehensive assessment of the banks that would come under its direct supervision, on which more below.

The choice of Article 127(6) as legal basis for the SSM Regulation, and its suitability for the extensive prudential supervisory authority the legislation conferred upon the ECB, had initially been a matter of much debate among legal experts and policymakers. Many were concerned – in line with views widely held in Germany, albeit against much accumulated experience outside that country – that having monetary policy and banking supervision under the same institutional roof would generate

---

84   For example, the European Parliament has access to the non-public records of proceedings of the ECB's Supervisory Board (ECB, 2024, section 5.1; Högenauer, 2023, page 127).

unmanageable conflicts of interest and ultimately undermine monetary policy independence[85]. At Germany's insistence[86], language was inserted stating that "*Article 127(6) TFEU could be amended to [...] go even further in the internal separation of decision-making on monetary policy and on supervision*" (SSM Regulation, Recital 85). As it turned out, and in line with Padoa-Schioppa's past insights, the coexistence of ECB banking supervision with the central bank's other activities in the same institution has proved to entail more apparent benefits than disadvantages, so far at least. It allows for fruitful exchanges between the supervisory staff and the ECB teams in charge of banking sector analysis in the respective directorates-general for macroprudential policy and financial stability, and for monetary policy[87]. The legal basis in Article 127(6) has also proved to be robust: for example, the SSM Regulation was challenged unsuccessfully before the German Constitutional Court, which in 2019 found it to "*not exceed the competences of the European Union*"[88].

---

85 Schäfer (2017, page 148) recounted that during the negotiations on the SSM Regulation in the second half of 2012, the German Finance Ministry "*was divided internally. While a smaller faction was willing to accept the ECB in this* [prudential] *role to entrust a highly credible institution with supervisory tasks, the majority view in the Finance Ministry forcefully opposed supervisory powers for the ECB. This larger group, which one senior official dubbed 'the puritans,' was at the helm. [...] The government eventually formed a preference against the ECB as banking supervisor. Following Schäuble's line, it staunchly advocated a separate institution in charge of banking supervisory powers, but not the ECB.*" Obviously, that German position, which contradicted the leaders' reference to Article 127(6) TFEU on 29 June 2012, did not prevail.

86 Tom Fairless, 'Germany Objects to EU Proposal for Restructuring Banks', *Wall Street Journal*, 10 July 2013, https://www.wsj.com/articles/SB10001424127887324425204578597213438213952.

87 The ECB's approach to such information sharing is to implement it on a need-to-know basis and only to an extent that it deems not to generate conflicts of interests, under the control of a dedicated mediation panel, as preferred alternative to a more rigid 'Chinese wall'; see ECA (2016), ECB comment #45 on page 124.

88 Federal Constitutional Court press release of 30 July 2019, 'If interpreted strictly, the framework for the European Banking Union does not exceed the competences of the European Union', https://www.bundesverfassungsgericht.de/SharedDocs/Pressemitteilungen/EN/2019/bvg19-052.html. Separately, in its Fininvest ruling of 19 December 2018 (Case

Transition to the handover of supervisory authority on 4 November 2014
Even though the final text of the SSM Regulation was only published in October 2013, its main features were set by the EU Council in mid-December 2012. From then until the effective transfer of supervisory authority scheduled for 4 November 2014, the ECB and other participants had nearly two years to prepare the transition to the new system. That complex endeavour involved three main parallel tracks.

First, the ECB had to define a practical model of prudential supervision that would make best use of the existing supervisory capabilities in the 19 countries of the euro area (including Latvia and Lithuania, which joined in January 2014 and January 2015 respectively) and resolve critical issues of division of labour between itself and the national authorities. Second, the ECB needed to build up its own capability, primarily in terms of recruiting staff for its supervisory arm and providing them with appropriate tools and resources (meanwhile, national supervisors also had to upgrade on multiple fronts). Third, the ECB had to make sure that the banks it took under supervision were worthy of their licenses, since it would become responsible for the latter. The SSM Regulation provided a path for that through its Article 33(4), which stipulated that the ECB should *"carry out a comprehensive assessment, including a balance-sheet assessment,"* of all the significant institutions for which it would become direct supervisor[89], and could to that effect require the soon-to-be-supervised entities and their national supervisors *"to provide all relevant information."* The comprehensive assessment, of

---

C-219/17), the EU Court of Justice confirmed that it had exclusive jurisdiction over ECB supervisory decisions made about significant institutions. Decisions made by national supervisors about less-significant institutions remain subject to national judicial review (Teixeira, 2020, page 235).

89 For the smaller banks that remained under direct national supervision, however, the ECB did not conduct a comprehensive assessment. It can thus be said that it took up the corresponding licensing legacy on trust.

course, had to be completed before the ECB's assumption of supervisory authority. Article 33(2) of the SSM Regulation gave the ECB an option to delay the entire process, in case the legislation's scheduled deadline of 4 November 2014 could not be met.

The first track, the definition of the supervisory model and the respective roles of the ECB and the pre-existing national supervisors, was the matter of a flurry of committees and working groups that determined the specifics of the new supervisory arrangements, but also created a degree of ownership of the new processes in the national agencies. It generated mutual knowledge among the individuals involved, in the respective national authorities and in the staff being hired at the ECB who had not previously much worked together, if at all. The tangible outcome of that collective effort was an ECB document published in April 2014, known as the SSM Framework Regulation (not to be confused with the SSM Regulation), counting no fewer than 153 articles on numerous matters of procedure[90].

One major innovation among these was the formation of joint supervisory teams for the supervision of significant institutions. Each team includes staff from the ECB and from national authorities, is led by an ECB coordinator, and has sub-coordinators at each of the relevant national supervisors. For example, the joint supervisory team for the euro area's largest bank by total assets, BNP Paribas[91], includes a coordinator (ie team leader) at the ECB in Frankfurt, who is not a French national, and sub-coordinators at the National Bank of Belgium in Brussels, the French Prudential Supervision and Resolution Authority in Paris, the Bank of Italy in Rome, the Financial Sector Supervisory

---

90   Regulation (EU) No. 468/2014 of the European Central Bank, of 16 April 2014.
91   BNP Paribas has held that top rank continuously since 2013 – thus throughout the existence of European banking supervision so far (source: *The Banker* database).

Commission in Luxembourg, the Dutch central bank in Amsterdam, and so on. Formally, all national authorities rank as equals in the team, including that of the country where the bank is headquartered. The ECB coordinator is solely responsible for proposing supervisory decisions to the ECB's Supervisory Board (and through it, to the Governing Council) but must report dissenting opinions in case there is no consensus among all sub-coordinators[92].

A corollary of this organisational choice, which was not self-evident at the outset and is by no means required by the SSM Regulation, is that the ECB has no supervisory staff based permanently outside Frankfurt. This has the advantage of reducing the scope for friction with national authorities on their respective home grounds, while not precluding direct access by the ECB to information on the ground. Specifically, ECB banking supervision organises time-limited onsite inspections of the banks under its watch. These are conducted by a team that is independent from the (offsite) joint supervisory team for the relevant bank, albeit in coordination with it (Dahlgren *et al*, 2023, page 40). Onsite inspections involve examiners from national authorities other than that of the country where they are conducted, including a head of mission selected by the ECB, either from its own staff or from a national authority. The ECB initiated 178 onsite inspections in 2023 (ECB, 2024, section 1.3.3).

As part of the same preparatory effort, the ECB had to work on multiple additional documents that would define the new supervisory mechanism and provide for appropriate coordination and accountability. As previously bargained with the European Parliament, it signed an agreement with it on scrutiny and information sharing (6

---

[92] By early 2023, a total 850 full-time equivalent staff from national authorities participated in joint supervisory teams alongside ECB employees (Dahlgren *et al*, 2023, page 12).

November 2013) and a memorandum of understanding on cooperation with the EU Council (4 and 11 December 2013). It adopted a decision on procedures for close cooperation with any non-euro-area countries that may join the banking union on a voluntary basis (31 January 2014); a decision on the procedure to appoint the ECB's representatives in the Supervisory Board (6 February 2014); a decision amending the rules of procedure for the ECB as a whole (19 February 2004); rules of procedure for the ECB Supervisory Board (31 March 2014); a decision establishing an Administrative Board of Review of the ECB's supervisory actions (14 April 2014); and a regulation establishing a Mediation Panel (2 June 2014)[93].

The second track was the ECB's internal recruitment and capacity build-up effort. In less than two years, the ECB recruited more than 1,000 new staff. Roughly three-quarters came from national authorities, which had incentives to get 'their' people into the new structures, but also disincentives to let go of their qualified supervisory experts. The remainder came from the outside job market. The ECB also rented and prepared offices, built up a statistical framework and information systems, and provided communication and other services to its fledgling supervisory arm. At a more intangible level, the ECB had to create a common culture and *esprit de corps* for its new supervisory staff, which could not be identical to that shared by its existing employees given the fundamental differences and operational separation between monetary

---

[93] For a review of the Administrative Board of Review's activity until late 2022, including details of individual cases, see ECB (2022b). About the Mediation Panel, the ECB website mentions that it is intended to resolve *"differences of views regarding an objection by the Governing Council to a draft decision of the Supervisory Board"* (see https://www.bankingsupervision.europa.eu/organisation/whoiswho/mediationpanel/html/index.en.html). All ECB annual reports on supervisory activities since 2015 have included the same sentence: *"Separation at the decision-making level did not raise concerns, and no intervention by the Mediation Panel was required"* (eg ECB, 2022a, 2023).

and banking supervisory tasks.

On 16 December 2013, the EU Council appointed Danièle Nouy, formerly head of the French banking supervisor, as chair of the ECB Supervisory Board and thus head of the new supervisory arm[94]. On 9 January 2014, the ECB announced the appointment of the four directors-general who would lead the supervisory staff: Korbinian Ibel (recruited from Commerzbank), Ramón Quintana (from the Bank of Spain), Jukka Vesala (from the Finnish supervisor) and Stefan Walter (from consultancy Ernst & Young). On 21 January, the EU Council appointed Sabine Lautenschläger, until then in charge of financial supervision at the German Bundesbank, to the ECB Executive Board, and the next day the ECB proposed her appointment as vice chair of its Supervisory Board, which was subsequently approved by the European Parliament on 12 February. On 6 March 2014, the ECB filled three of its four additional seats on the Supervisory Board by appointing Ignazio Angeloni, Julie Dickson and Sirkka Hämäläinen as its representatives[95]. Throughout 2014, the ECB's senior supervisory staff would devote much of their time and activity to hiring more employees, while simultaneously establishing the new organisation's working practices and coordinating the massive effort that was the comprehensive assessment.

The third track was the comprehensive assessment itself, including asset quality review and stress testing, of the banks that would come under the ECB's direct supervision. This was a massive exercise of data analysis and disclosure, which the ECB had to carry out without having its full team in place, with overwhelming practical reliance on incumbent national supervisors, resulting in numerous compromises and significant parts of

---

[94] Ms Nouy was viewed as frontrunner for the position since at least February 2013; see Alex Barker and Michael Steen, 'ECB told to double its manpower', *Financial Times*, 4 February 2013, https://www.ft.com/content/8c178adc-6ed4-11e2-8189-00144feab49a.

[95] The fourth initial ECB representative, Luc Coene, was appointed in early 2015.

the analytical work being outsourced to private-sector consultants. The ECB was mindful of not unnecessarily antagonising the national supervisors in the process because it needed their constructive engagement on other aspects of its institutional build-up, which created potentially perverse incentives for at least temporary forbearance. In 2014, the ECB assessed a total of 130 banking groups, complemented in 2015 by assessments of nine additional banks, plus a renewed assessment of the four main Greek banks following the turmoil that affected Greece in the summer of 2015. The 2014 exercise resulted in the identification of capital shortfalls as of end-2013 in 25 banking groups. Of these, 12 raised enough capital during 2014 to offset their shortfalls by the time of publication of the results in late October.

With the benefit of hindsight, the 2014 comprehensive assessment can be viewed as a qualified success. It avoided the obvious shortcomings of previous comparable EU-wide exercises, namely the stress tests in 2010 (coordinated by CEBS) and 2011 (coordinated by the newly established EBA), which had failed to identify problems in banks that failed shortly afterwards. The comprehensive assessment also avoided the pitfalls of the 2011-2012 capital exercise, also coordinated by the EBA, which had marked the value of banks' sovereign debt holdings to market and thus entailed a risk of exacerbating the bank-sovereign vicious circle, even though the immediate effect was mitigated by the ECB's liquidity provision through the long-term refinancing operations programme of late 2011. It led to significant amounts of capital raising from the market by banks which did not want to be identified as exhibiting capital shortfalls, under either the current or future ('fully-loaded Basel III') definition of capital requirements[96].

---

96   Basel III refers to the third accord of the Basel Committee on Banking Supervision, first agreed in late 2010 and complemented since then, which sets international standards for bank capital, leverage, liquidity and stress testing. 'Fully loaded' refers to the application of requirements as applicable after the end of the protracted transition period also set out by Basel III.

The comprehensive assessment demonstrated the ECB's capacity to corral the national supervisors into a highly complex process, with more authority than the EBA had been able to wield given the latter's weaker legislative mandate and considerably more limited resources. The ECB also met the deadline assigned for it, and did not have to use the above-mentioned option to extend the timetable under Article 33(2) of the SSM Regulation. Even so, the ECB could not practically screen all assets and commitments of all scrutinised banks with a uniformly high level of rigour, and had to make compromises. As subsequent developments demonstrated, for a number of banks, the comprehensive assessment's official findings underestimated the extent of hidden losses and the corresponding capital shortfalls. This was notably the case for several banks in Germany (eg HSH Nordbank, Nord/LB, and by some accounts also Deutsche Bank) and in Italy (eg Banca Popolare di Vicenza, Veneto Banca, Carige, and Monte dei Paschi di Siena).

Some observers did not view the 2014 exercise as substantially different from previous failed approaches to euro-area banking sector cleanup. Bank capital expert Morris Goldstein wrote some time later: *"I believe that the main conclusions of the 2014 EU-wide bank stress test are not credible"* (Goldstein, 2017, page 57)[97]. Even though this and other similar judgments made at the time can be viewed as harsh, the comprehensive assessment did fall short of a cathartic clean break

---

[97] Goldstein's assessment rested on four main points, on which he referred to other critical analysts. First, the comprehensive assessment did not include a leverage ratio, ie the adequacy of the banks' capital was only measured against risk-weighted assets, with inherent scope for gaming the risk weighting, and not against total (unweighted) assets. Second, the stress tests did not include a deflationary scenario, which appeared probable at the time and would have had an adverse impact on bank profitability. Third, the possibility of counting deferred tax assets and tax credits as capital made some banks' headline capital numbers artificially high. Fourth, the small overall capital shortage supported suspicions that calculations, including assessments of asset values, might had been manipulated in order to attain a desired outcome set *ex ante*.

that would instantly have restored trust in euro-area banks. The ECB's approach in 2014 can be labelled a form of selective forbearance, generally rigorous but with several exceptions made. It was the start, not the end, of a cycle of exacting supervision, in which the ECB requested and achieved much de-risking and balance sheet strengthening from the banks under its direct supervision in the years that immediately followed.

Supervisory practice since November 2014

Prudential supervisors, similarly to various other government agencies, are judged largely on the basis of their failures; their greatest successes typically happen behind closed doors and remain unsung, at least in the public space. Indeed, as argued in chapter 3, it was the comprehensive failure of national supervisors that led to the decision to establish European banking supervision in mid-2012[98]. The ECB, by contrast, appears to have been proactive and to have requested banks under its direct supervision to strengthen their balance sheets and liquidity positions to the extent needed, in line with the phasing-in of the more demanding requirements enshrined in the newly harmonised EU regulatory rulebook adopted in 2013. As previously observed, it is difficult to disentangle the impact of the ECB's supervisory efforts from that of the improved regulatory framework, namely the EU Capital Requirements Regulation (CRR) of 2013 and its successive updates, and from the banks' own-initiative efforts to shore up their financial soundness. CRR represented the first time that the EU gave itself a

---

98   Of course, not every bank failure is a supervisory failure, and supervisors are not the only ones failing whenever a bank fails. Still, bank failures are generally how supervisory failures come to be revealed.

genuine single rulebook for bank capital and liquidity requirements[99]. A revision enacted in 2019 included the introduction of a minimum leverage ratio (of regulatory capital over unweighted assets, thus less prone to manipulation through biased risk models), which became binding in mid-2021. A further revision in 2024 constrained the ability of banks to weigh certain assets as very low risk.

In multiple cases, the ECB has pushed weak banks to raise fresh capital, often at the expense of shareholders whose equity stakes were correspondingly diluted, and sometimes with the help of various forms of government support. These cases included:

- The four main Greek banks, recapitalised in late 2015 after a traumatic national sequence of events that year;
- HSH Nordbank, a German regional bank whose local-government shareholders supported a balance-sheet cleanup in 2016 and which, to meet European Commission state-aid control conditions, had to sell to private-sector shareholders in 2018;
- Monte dei Paschi di Siena, which became majority owned by the Italian government through a 'precautionary' recapitalisation in 2017, and painfully completed a further round of equity raising at the end of 2022[100];
- Carige, another Italian problem case that was shored up by a consortium of the country's larger banks and subsequently acquired

---

99 The idea of a single rulebook, pioneered by Padoa-Schioppa in the early 2000s, became a matter of EU consensus in the aftermath of the Lehman Brothers failure (Larosière, 2009). The European Commission's initial proposal for CRR, published on 20 July 2011, predated the banking union by nearly a year.

100 The Italian state participated in that round in proportion to its prior shareholding of 64 percent (it has since reduced it). See Silvia Sciorilli Borrelli, 'Monte dei Paschi cash call 93% covered but shareholders shy away', *Financial Times*, 31 October 2022, https://www.ft.com/content/924b8892-cd95-46f0-97c0-8468ee6e9660.

in 2022 by mid-sized Banca BPER;
- Nord/LB, yet another troubled German regional bank that was recapitalised in 2019 by its public-sector shareholders.

In other cases, fresh capital was insufficient or unavailable, even with the support of public funds, and the ECB had to declare banks 'failing or likely to fail' under the EU Bank Recovery and Resolution Directive of 2014, on which more in the next chapter. These cases included two mid-sized banks in the Italian region of Venetia, Veneto Banca and Banca Popolare di Vicenza, in 2017; and also in 2017, Spain's Banco Popular Español during an idiosyncratic episode of liquidity stress in the midst of a process of being (potentially) acquired by a competitor. All these appear to have been legacy cases of banks that the ECB had already identified as problem-ridden by the time of the comprehensive assessment in 2014. It may be argued that the ECB should have addressed their problems more quickly and forcefully[101]. The problems at these banks did not first appear under the ECB's own watch, however. An expert group commissioned by the ECB, in its review of the practice of European banking supervision after 2014, *"found no evidence of favourable scores having been assigned to banks that subsequently failed"* (Dahlgren *et al*, 2023, page 29)[102].

The ECB has gradually fostered more rigorous practices in the

---

101   In the case of Monte dei Paschi, there were media allegations based on leaked internal documents that the ECB should have designated the bank as 'failing or likely to fail' in 2016. See Elisa Martinuzzi, 'What the ECB Didn't Say About Monte Paschi's Bailout', *Bloomberg Opinion*, 30 June 2019, https://www.bloomberg.com/graphics/2019-opinion-monte-paschi/. These claims also raised the question of whether the Single Resolution Board should have done so under its own backup authority (Véron, 2019).

102   The ECB clarified to the author that, while the expert group's members did not have generalised access to the confidential supervisory scores of all banks, they could review past scores for those banks that subsequently failed.

calculation of capital ratios, particularly in two areas that featured highly in the criticisms of its comprehensive assessment in 2014. On non-performing loans, the ECB established a group in 2015 that produced detailed guidance in 2017 with an addendum in 2018, to ensure better provisioning of doubtful assets. On risk weighting, the ECB between 2016 and 2021 conducted a large-scale assessment of risk models used by 65 large banking groups, dubbed the Targeted Review of Internal Models, to ensure a degree of consistency (ECB, 2022a, section 1.3.2.2)[103]. The head of ECB banking supervision subsequently described the challenge of non-performing loans as "*a huge legacy problem in the banking system when we took over supervision*" and the targeted review of internal models as "*the largest project conducted by ECB Banking Supervision in coordination with NCAs* [national competent authorities] *to date*" (Enria, 2023a). An empirical study focused on Germany found that European banking supervision actually resulted in more equal treatment of banks, with tighter standards than under the prior national supervisory regime (Haselmann *et al*, 2022).

Beyond coaxing banks into raising more capital, the ECB has also fostered changes in the corporate governance of several of them. These actions, however, tend to be even less observable from public information than those described previously. They often took the form of behind-the-scenes communications by the ECB to the relevant national authorities, or non-public suggestions made to the banks themselves. In the case of the German Savings Banks Group, the media reported joint action by the ECB and the German supervisory authority BaFin, resulting in the creation of a new institutional protection fund that is

---

[103] Supervised banks have occasionally disclosed the impact of ECB requirements on their risk modelling: see KBC Group press release of 10 August 2023, 'KBC Group: Second-quarter result of 966 million euros', https://newsroom.kbc.com/kbc-group-second-quarter-result-of-966-million-euros.

expected to mitigate the kind of slow and uncertain decision-making within the group's elaborate structures, which delayed, for instance, the recapitalisation of Nord/LB as mentioned above[104]. In other cases of bank-governance changes since November 2014, there is no way to infer from publicly available information the extent to which the ECB may have played a decisive role. Examples include governance improvements in Spanish savings banks, including the appointment of professional independent non-executive board members (a process that had started several years before European banking supervision), several steps of streamlining of the Austrian Raiffeisen banking group in 2017 and 2021, and governance adjustments at France's Crédit Mutuel in 2023. The former head of ECB banking supervision has commented that friction with supervised banks *"tends to be most intense when we raise concerns on governance and the sustainability of banks' business models"*[105].

At a higher, system-wide level, the ECB demonstrated its capacity to act forcefully in response to the shock of the COVID-19 pandemic in the spring of 2020. The ECB publicly asked the banks it supervised to suspend dividend distributions and share buybacks to preserve capital in face of possible waves of pandemic-induced bankruptcies. In this, the ECB was ahead of peers such as the Bank of England and the US

---

104 Andreas Kröner, 'Angriff auf die Sparkassen: Bafin und EZB fordern Umbau des Sicherungssystems', *Handelsblatt*, 28 May 2020, https://www.handelsblatt.com/finanzen/banken-versicherungen/banken/finanzaufsicht-angriff-auf-die-sparkassen-bafin-und-ezb-fordern-umbau-des-sicherungssystems/25864786.html. The Savings Banks Group's apex entity, the Deutscher Sparkassen- und Giroverband, expressed displeasure at the fact that such information had made it into the public domain (*Reuters*, 'Finanzaufsicht fordert extra Fonds für Sparkassen-Rettung', Reuters, 28 May 2020, https://www.reuters.com/article/deutschland-sparkassen-institutssicherun-idDEKBN23415Q/). In three successive replies to written European Parliament questions (respectively on 3 July 2020, 21 July 2020 and 21 July 2021), the ECB declined to provide any further details.

105 European Central Bank, 'Interview with Andrea Enria, Chair of the Supervisory Board of the ECB, Supervision Newsletter', 15 November 2023, https://www.bankingsupervision.europa.eu/press/interviews/date/2023/html/ssm.in231115~258ce989fa.en.html.

Federal Reserve[106]. The ECB near-simultaneously relaxed some capital requirements to mitigate the risk of pro-cyclical shock amplification, and delayed some of its own supervisory proceeding deadlines in order to give the banks breathing space[107]. That episode provided the first practical demonstration of the ability of European banking supervision to make crisis-management decisions without the concerns about competitive distortions and stigma effects that had crippled the actions of national supervisors between 2007 and 2012 (Teixeira, 2021). As it turned out, the fears about waves of corporate bankruptcies did not materialise, thanks in no small part to massive fiscal interventions by euro-area countries to support credit. It is still notable, however, that the pandemic shock, and in 2022 the consequences of Russia's full-scale invasion of Ukraine and of the subsequent energy crisis, have not resulted in any visible banking sector distress, let alone failures[108].

The concept of the joint supervisory teams has successfully passed the test of time. An in-depth study by political scientist Jonathan Zeitlin, based on numerous interviews with supervisory staff, both at the ECB and in the national supervisory authorities of a half dozen countries, observed that the system provides effective incentives to its participants to work together constructively. In Zeitlin's words,

---

106   ECB press release of 27 March 2020, 'ECB asks banks not to pay dividends until at least October 2020', https://www.bankingsupervision.europa.eu/press/pr/date/2020/html/ssm.pr200327~d4d8f81a53.en.html. See also John Miller and Sinead Cruise, 'Euro zone banks ditch dividends to build coronavirus war chest', *Reuters*, 30 March 2020, https://www.reuters.com/article/health-coronavirus-bank-dividends/euro-zone-banks-ditch-dividends-to-build-coronavirus-war-chest-idUKL8N2BN24Y. The ECB lifted its restrictions on dividends in September 2021 (ECB, 2022a).
107   ECB press release of 12 March 2020, 'ECB Banking Supervision provides temporary capital and operational relief in reaction to coronavirus', ECB Banking Supervision provides temporary capital and operational relief in reaction to coronavirus.
108   Leaving aside, of course, euro-area affiliates of Russian banks in 2022, such as Sberbank as mentioned below.

European banking supervision is best described neither as a *"centralized hierarchy"* nor as a *"polyarchic network"*, even though it has features of both, but rather as an *"experimentalist organization"* that seeks to accommodate diversity by adapting common rules and procedures to the specificities of individual banks, and revises them regularly through peer review of implementation experience at multiple levels (Zeitlin, 2023). Whereas it is possible to imagine that the interactions between the ECB and national supervisors have generated numerous frictions and disagreements over the years, remarkably few of these have emerged into the public domain as blatant signals of dysfunction. The main such case was the Bank of Italy's concerns in the mid-2010s about what it viewed as overly aggressive demands for capital strengthening by the ECB at the time[109], but these concerns appear to have subsided in more recent years.

More broadly, the build-up of European banking supervision has enabled the gradual emergence of a shared supervisory culture between the ECB and participating national supervisors. This also applies increasingly to the direct national supervision of smaller banks[110].

---

109 See eg Patrick Henry, 'Bank of Italy Letter Slams "Arbitrary" ECB Over Capital Demands,' *Bloomberg*, 21 September 2015 https://www.bloomberg.com/news/articles/2015-09-21/bank-of-italy-letter-slams-arbitrary-ecb-over-capital-demands.

110 As previously described, the boundary between 'significant institutions' directly supervised by the ECB and 'less-significant institutions' directly supervised by national authorities is of structural importance in the organisation of European banking supervision, but the view that the latter effectively escape ECB oversight has become increasingly mistaken. Aside from the already mentioned joint work of the ECB and BaFin on the German IPSs, European banking supervision has introduced categories of 'high-impact' and 'high-risk' less-significant institutions, both under closer watch by the ECB than other small banks, including those specifically designated in recent EU legislation as 'small non-complex institutions,' for which some of the prudential requirements are simplified. The ECB first published the list of 92 high-impact less-significant institutions in 2022, with €1.8 trillion in aggregate assets, of which two-thirds were in France and Germany (ECB, 2022a); the next year the list had grown to 97 banks with total assets slightly over €2 trillion (ECB, 2023). The ECB understandably does not publish the list of high-risk less-significant institutions.

Simultaneously, the new architecture has facilitated the collection and analysis of information and data about banks, which used to be very hard to compare on a cross-border basis. This harmonisation effort has enabled a single methodology known as the Supervisory Review and Evaluation Process (SREP), to classify all supervised banks into risk levels known as SREP scores (from 1 to 4), functionally comparable to the Uniform Financial Institutions Rating System (known as CAMELS ratings) used by bank prudential supervisors in the United States[111]. The ECB in 2022 commissioned an independent review of the SREP, highlighting its awareness of the risk that the process might become formulaic and miss emerging risk factors (Dahlgren *et al*, 2023).

Through its publications and interactions with the European Parliament (and to a lesser extent, with national parliaments in the banking union countries), ECB banking supervision has established a commendably high level of transparency in relation to its general policies and operations, while following the supervisory practice of not communicating about individual cases[112]. Progress has been slower but is now also underway in terms of providing comparable public information about supervised entities. Data on significant institutions published through the EBA portal has become more comprehensive over the years, both in terms of metrics disclosed for each reporting entity and in terms of scope of reporting groups, which now includes nearly all significant institutions. For less significant institutions, the ECB has

---

111   CAMELS stands for Capital, Assets, Management capability, Earnings, Liquidity, Sensitivity to market risk. Whereas SREP is an EU-wide methodology based on EBA guidelines, the setup of European banking supervision in the euro area allows for a greater consistency than across other EU member states.

112   For example, based on the methodology of a 2013 study of national supervisors, Högenauer (2023) found the ECB scoring higher than average in all categories and better than all euro-area national supervisors that were included in the 2013 research.

increasingly disclosed figures at an aggregate level (ECB, 2020, 2022c)[113].

As for individual data, the EBA, with ECB support, is at time of writing planning implementation of a so-called Pillar 3 data hub (where Pillar 3 refers to due disclosures defined by the Basel framework). This is set to become operational by 2025 and would bring the EU closer to global best practice[114], especially in the United States where authorities provide detailed quarterly 'call reports' immediately accessible for all banks[115]. That protracted progress in transparency is a reflection of the differences in data reporting by banks, which the ECB has only started to tackle relatively recently[116]. One related challenge is that EU legislation has not harmonised accounting standards for unlisted banks, unlike in many jurisdictions around the world (and some individual EU countries), where all banks have to use the same accounting standards as publicly listed companies.

Comparison with the United States

In terms of aggregate banking assets, the world's top three jurisdictions under integrated banking supervision are now, in size order, China, the

---

113 See also ECB quarterly aggregated statistics with starting point in Q2 2020, published from May 2023; ECB press release of 10 May 2023, 'ECB publishes supervisory banking statistics on less significant institutions', https://www.bankingsupervision.europa.eu/press/pr/date/2023/html/ssm.pr230510~1752171746.en.html.
114 See the EBA Pillar 3 data hub, https://www.eba.europa.eu/activities/single-rulebook/regulatory-activities/transparency-and-pillar-3/pillar-3-data-hub.
115 Access is channelled via a portal maintained jointly by the relevant US supervisory agencies through their common grouping, the Federal Financial Institutions Examination Council. See https://cdr.ffiec.gov/public/ManageFacsimiles.aspx. US call reports contain more financial information than is planned for inclusion in the EBA's Pillar 3 data hub, especially for smaller banks and credit unions.
116 ECB press release of 17 December 2021, 'ECB moves towards harmonising statistical reporting to ease burden for banks and improve analysis', https://www.ecb.europa.eu/press/pr/date/2021/html/ecb.pr211217~168928ae51.en.html. See also Enria (2023b).

banking union and the United States[117]. A major overhaul of the Chinese financial supervisory system was implemented in 2023, and it is too early to assess the implications of the resulting new architecture. Conversely, it is instructive to compare European banking supervision with its American peer.

In the United States, the functional equivalent of European banking supervision is the supervisory cluster formed by the Federal Reserve System, the Office of the Comptroller of the Currency within the US Department of the Treasury, the Federal Deposit Insurance Corporation (FDIC) in its capacity as principal supervisor of a number of (generally smaller) banks, and the banking supervisory authorities of individual states and territories, eg the New York State Department of Financial Services[118]. In addition, the US has a parallel system for credit unions, administered by the National Credit Union Administration and the respective state-level authorities[119].

For supervisory purposes, the Federal Reserve System consists of 12 regional Federal Reserve Banks and the Board of Governors in

---

117   Because the US financial system is more markets-based, its size measured by banking assets is smaller than that of the euro area, despite the latter's economy being smaller by aggregate GDP. At the end of 2023, aggregate assets of US commercial banks were $23 trillion (ca. €21 trillion; from the Federal Reserve's FRED database; not including about $2 trillion in credit unions). Significant institutions in the banking union had aggregate total assets slightly above €25 trillion, and less-significant institutions represented 15.4 percent of the aggregate total (excluding financial market infrastructures), implying a total of nearly €30 trillion for the whole banking union area at end-2023 (ECB, 2024). By this same measure, China overtook the euro area in the mid-2010s (eg Schoenmaker and Véron, 2016, page 12), and is now considerably larger with around €54 trillion in total banking assets at end-2023 (*Xinhua*, 'China's banking sector assets up in 2023', 26 January 2024, https://global.chinadaily.com.cn/a/202401/26/WS65b3203aa3105f21a507e849.html).

118   The US supervisory landscape is analysed in more detail in CRS (2020).

119   In the euro area, a few countries have credit unions that are supervised outside the remit of European banking supervision (and of EU capital requirements legislation), but these are negligible in size: the largest by far is Ireland, with total credit-union assets slightly under €20 billion in 2022. By comparison, the assets of US credit unions at the same date were

Washington DC. The Board has statutory authority for bank regulation and supervision, but it has:

> *"delegated day-to-day supervision of state member banks and bank holding companies to the individual Federal Reserve Banks, subject to various types of continued Federal Reserve Board involvement, which includes (i) Board oversight of the Federal Reserve Bank's supervisory activities, (ii) an informal advisory role for Board staff in material supervisory determinations (particularly with respect to larger banks), (iii) a formal, programmatic role for Board staff in defining and implementing supervisory priorities and exercises through Board-controlled supervisory groups (e.g., the Large Institution Supervision Coordinating Committee [...]) and (iv) a formal Board role in certain key decisions (e.g., whether to approve certain applications and/or initiate enforcement action)"* (Newell, 2023, pages 8-9).

Since the Dodd-Frank Act of 2010, the boards of directors of the regional Federal Reserve Banks have had no formal oversight role over the latter's supervisory activities, even though in practice there are indications that the insulation is not complete (Judge, 2023, pages 8-9). Within these broad parameters, the respective roles of the Board and the regional Reserve Banks in supervisory decision-making are not described as specifically in Federal Reserve publications as in the equivalent ECB publications (such as the ECB Annual Report on supervisory activities), even in the unprecedented disclosures that the

---

about 100 times greater. As a consequence, comparing credit institutions in the banking union with banks and credit unions in the United States comes close to an apples-to-apples comparison. See Lehmann and Véron (2021, page 15), and the European Network of Credit Unions website, http://www.creditunionnetwork.eu/cus_in_europe.

Federal Reserve made in May 2023 following the collapse of Silicon Valley Bank (FRB, 2023; Newell, 2023, pages 11-12).

Overall, the US supervisory framework is somewhat more complex and fragmented than in the euro area because of the multiplicity of federal agencies involved, different categories of supervised institutions[120], and the fact that they can be chartered at either the state or federal level. Focusing on the comparison between Federal Reserve banking supervision and European banking supervision, there are features of greater centralisation on either side depending on the perspective adopted. For example, in the banking union, all joint supervisory team coordinators for significant institutions are ECB employees based in Frankfurt. Their functional equivalents at the Federal Reserve ('examiners in charge') are typically employed by and located at the relevant regional Reserve Bank, while conducting their supervisory tasks under the authority of the Federal Reserve Board.

As already mentioned, assessing supervisory effectiveness is hard, in either absolute or relative terms. An intriguing comparative perspective on the respective performance of European and US banking supervision was provided in 2023, however, because both jurisdictions were subject to broadly similar trajectories in terms of rapid increases in policy rates following a long period of low or negative rates, creating challenges for banks especially in terms of interest-rate risk and business-model risk. The contrast between the corresponding casualties in America, with the high-profile failures of Silicon Valley Bank and Signature Bank in March 2023, and the absence of such cases in the euro area, put US supervisors under a relatively unflattering spotlight. It is notable, in this respect, that *"sensitivities to shocks in interest rates and credit spreads"* was listed by

---

120 Some state-chartered banks are members of the Federal Reserve System while others are not, and credit unions are under a separate framework.

the ECB among *"key vulnerabilities"* in a document about its supervisory priorities published in late 2021 (ECB, 2021), while no similar statement was made at the time by US counterparts. In the same vein, the independent review of the SREP, drafted before the Silicon Valley Bank fiasco, noted that *"the ECB's SREP includes elements that are not present in other jurisdictions, such as a dedicated assessment of business model risks, which is a strength"* (Dahlgren et al, 2023, page 29).

Overall assessment

All things considered, the prudential supervision component of the European banking union project appears robust and complete at the time of this writing[121]. Together with the decisive step towards a single prudential rulebook represented by the CRR, it can be viewed as a fulfilment of the most ambitious articulations of European banking policy integration outlined by Tommaso Padoa-Schioppa and others in the late twentieth century, as related in chapter 2. It is not even clear that further legislative integration or centralisation of the supervisory framework (eg more direct ECB supervision of smaller banks) is desirable, assuming the specific challenges posed by IPSs are appropriately addressed. The ECB Supervisory Board, with its 34 members (ECB, 2024, section 5.6.1), is unwieldy compared to the main decision-making bodies of other banking supervisors around the world, but that has not appeared to undermine its decision-making activity so far. Concerns about potential conflicts of interest between monetary

---

121 In addition to other sources mentioned, this assessment takes into account the reports published, among others, by the European Commission (2017b, 2023) and by the European Court of Auditors in 2016 (ECA, 2016) and 2023 (on the narrower issue of bank credit risk supervision; ECA, 2023). The assessment of supervisory integration within the banking union as *"complete"* is made holistically and notwithstanding lingering discrepancies in national legal frameworks (Bassani, 2020).

policy and banking supervision within the ECB, which were prominent in the decision-making phase of 2012-2013, have largely subsided. Notably, the ECB in the early 2020s compared favourably to the US Federal Reserve's subpar performance at addressing financial-stability risks generated by monetary policy decisions[122], suggesting the ECB was more effective at separating the two functions. In short, the experience of the past decade has not brought to light any strong reason to consider major changes to the SSM Regulation.

European banking supervision so far appears to have been broadly independent, even though compromises had to be made in its early build-up phase, particularly during the comprehensive assessment of 2014. The ECB has built a generally constructive relationship with national supervisors. In at least some countries, the national supervisor may also have been able to enhance its own independence from national political or industry pressures, compared with the pre-2012 period, thanks to integration in the European banking supervision framework. European banking supervision has practically established a supervisory level playing field across countries in the banking union, and does not appear to have been captured by industry interests. The latter assessment is corroborated by occasional complaints from the supervised banks about the demanding requirements and expectations placed on them[123].

The general success of European banking supervision to date may be ascribed to a confluence of several factors. It has a solid legal basis in

---

122   Bill Dudley, 'What the Fed Missed in Its Bank Crisis Confessional', *Bloomberg Opinion*, 10 May 2023, https://www.bloomberg.com/opinion/articles/2023-05-10/what-the-fed-missed-in-its-bank-crisis-confessional.

123   For example, Sarah White, Owen Walker, Laura Noonan and Martin Arnold, 'Europe's bank bosses push back against perceived ECB intrusion', *Financial Times*, 4 November 2022, https://www.ft.com/content/c73e9018-5528-4d9e-829b-af74f6650fef; *Reuters*, 'Deutsche Bank Joins Industry Criticism of ECB', 9 November 2022, https://www.reuters.com/markets/europe/deutsche-bank-joins-recent-industry-criticism-ecb-2022-11-09/.

Article 127(6) TFEU. The drafting of the SSM Regulation in the summer of 2012, despite having been done under extreme time pressure, has turned out to have been of high quality. The incubation of the new structure within the ECB, an independent and resourceful organisation, has been of critical importance, as have generally fortunate appointments of key officials and executives. A common culture and sense of mission appear to have emerged among ECB banking supervision staff, despite the difficulties inherent in building a large supranational organisation.

That positive assessment comes with two caveats. First, the past is no guide to the future. There can be no certainty that European banking supervision will maintain a high level of performance in the years ahead. There is a risk that the very perception of success may breed harmful complacency. Second, most of those who dreamt of European banking supervision in the last third of the twentieth century did so with the underlying implication that regulatory and supervisory integration would be enough to form a fully resilient supranational banking policy framework[124]. The experience of the euro-area crisis demonstrated that such reasoning underestimated the magnitude of the challenge, as it neglected the possibility both of systemic banking solvency crises and of sovereign defaults, and therefore the associated bank-sovereign vicious circle. As a consequence, even with complete and effective European banking supervision, the banking union as defined by the euro-area summit statement on 29 June 2012, namely the project to break the vicious circle between banks and sovereigns, remains fragile and incomplete.

---

124   As mentioned earlier in this text, Vives (1992) was a notable exception as he articulated the need for a crisis management and deposit insurance authority alongside a European supervisor.

5 UNFINISHED WORK: SOVEREIGN EXPOSURES AND CRISIS-INTERVENTION FRAMEWORK

Moving away from the three-pillar narrative

From its beginning in 2012, the banking union has been described in EU official communications as having three pillars, resting on the common foundation of the single rulebook. Of these pillars, the first two were established early on – European banking supervision as described in the previous chapter, and the so-called single resolution mechanism as described below. The third, European deposit insurance, is yet to come. This framing has been accepted and adopted near-ubiquitously by analysts and observers. It has the advantage of simplicity, and it initially provided an elegant way to sidestep any discussion of integrated deposit insurance while making progress on other fronts.

However, for reasons detailed in the rest of this chapter, the three-pillar narrative has become increasingly unhelpful. First, it omits the critical issue of banks' concentrated domestic sovereign exposures, one of the drivers of the bank-sovereign vicious circle that the banking union project is intended to address. Second, the three-pillar story is often told in a way that implies that the resolution (second) pillar is fully formed and functional. Despite progress on multiple fronts, experience since 2015 suggests it is not. Third, more broadly, the three-pillar idea introduces an artificial separation between resolution and deposit insurance, which was temporarily useful in the circumstances of 2012-2014, but stands at odds with longstanding experience that has demonstrated the interdependencies between the two, within the broader bank crisis-intervention framework.

Instead of pillars, this chapter focuses on the two main challenges that stand on the way of completing the banking union. As argued in the previous chapter, prudential supervision is not one of them. The first challenge is concentrated domestic sovereign exposures. The second challenge bundles together all matters of bank crisis management and resolution, which must be considered holistically ic including bank resolution, deposit insurance and other elements such as state-aid control.

This alternative framing results from both practical experience and policy discussions about the completion of banking union over the last decade. After many iterations, reports, working groups and negotiation breakdowns, it has become increasingly clear that the two challenges are ultimately related and interdependent. In time-honoured Brussels fashion, each has come to be captured into a four-letter set of initials: respectively, RTSE for regulatory treatment of sovereign exposures, and CMDI for crisis management and deposit insurance[125]. The lesson of the past eight years is that trying to tackle these two challenges sequentially or separately is bound to fail. In other words, a 'grand-bargain' approach is needed that addresses them both.

This 'RTSE + CMDI' framing is not just the result of *ad-hoc*

---

125 Further illustrating the intricacies of four-letter initialisms in Brussels, the European Commission in March 2024 published a European Defence Industrial Strategy, suggesting that EDIS is no longer to refer to the European Deposit Insurance Scheme, a meaning it had since 2015. See European Commission press release of 5 March 2024, 'First ever defence industrial strategy and a new defence industry programme to enhance Europe's readiness and security', https://ec.europa.eu/commission/presscorner/detail/en/ip_24_1321.

interactions in obscure committees. It reflects the fundamentals of the bank-sovereign vicious circle. Through concentrated domestic sovereign exposures, banks are directly affected by sovereign weakness, and through implicit and explicit guarantees embedded in the crisis-intervention framework (including, but far from limited to, the explicit guarantee of deposits), sovereigns are directly affected by bank failures. Indirect linkages, through the national macroeconomic environment that may be negatively affected by both national sovereign credit and banking sector fragilities, are obviously also significant. That observation, however, does not negate the policy centrality of addressing the direct linkages that feed the bank-sovereign vicious circle most powerfully. The indirect (macroeconomic) linkages exist in a similar manner, at the sub-national or local level, in all other jurisdictions with integrated banking systems, to an extent that is of course correlated with fiscal decentralisation and banking sector fragmentation. By contrast, the direct linkages, namely national contingent sovereign liabilities linked to crisis intervention and concentrated domestic sovereign exposures, are largely specific to the present-day banking union[126].

The rest of this chapter looks at sovereign exposures and then crisis management and deposit insurance, and concludes on the interplay between the respective RTSE and CMDI agendas.

Concentrated domestic sovereign exposures

The challenge posed by concentrated domestic sovereign exposures is specific to the euro area as a monetary union. In a unitary jurisdiction

---

126   The present-day United States provides an example of a fully integrated system in which the indirect linkages still exist and especially affect local banks, but the direct linkages have effectively disappeared.

with its own currency, it is natural for banks to own sizeable portfolios of domestic-currency-denominated securities of (and loans to) the government, which in principle are the highest-quality local liquid assets they can hold, aside from deposits (reserves) at the central bank. These assets are collectively referred to as domestic sovereign exposures[127]. In a supranational monetary union that encompasses several countries and where there is no large-scale permanent issuance of supranational (federal) debt, the question arises of which mix of national sovereign exposures a bank may hold – in other words, how much exposure should it have to the different countries within that multi-country area.

If the monetary union is viewed as permanent, there is no self-evident reason why a bank's choice of exposures to the union's different sovereigns should be dependent on the specific country where it happens to be headquartered. In practice, however, euro-area banks, though with wide variations across individual cases, tend to hold most of their euro-area sovereign exposures in the country from which they originated and are registered, or their home country. In other words, their 'home bias', defined as the ratio of home-country (or domestic) sovereign exposures to total euro-area sovereign exposures, tends to be high[128]. The reasons for this home bias are debated (see for example Altavilla *et al*, 2017), but its existence and persistence are undeniable, as documented by data collected by the EBA for its annual transparency exercise (even though this data only includes the scope of banking prudential supervision, and therefore leaves out any sovereign exposures held in banking groups' insurance subsidiaries).

Table 1 summarises the data, covering nearly all euro-area-head-

---

[127] The definition of sovereign exposures used here aligns with EU practice with reference to general government, including debt of local government and non-commercial government entities.
[128] There are other possible definitions of home bias; the one used here is specifically suited for the debate about banks' concentrated sovereign exposures in the euro-area context.

quartered significant institutions[129]. The median significant euro-area bank displays a home bias of 71 percent, ie more than seven-tenths of its euro-area sovereign exposures are to its home country. The median capital coverage ratio is 89 percent, ie the median bank's Tier-1 capital would be reduced by close to half in the severe but plausible scenario of a domestic sovereign credit event that would result in a 50 percent haircut[130]. For a number of banks the ratio is considerably higher, as illustrated by the higher average. In Spain, the median is above 200 percent: in other words, a sovereign default with a 50 percent haircut would directly render more than half of the country's significant banks insolvent. Italy is not far from that level.

Table 2 shows the same metrics for a subsample of the same banks which is held fixed over time, including most of the largest ones, which reported similar data in mid-2016 (missing several mid-sized Italian and Spanish banks, thus the discrepancies compared to Table 1)[131]. The table indicates a decrease in home bias during the period, but not by nearly enough to view the problem as self-resolving. The much more pronounced decrease in capital coverage ratios arises from an increase in capital levels, rather than a decrease in domestic sovereign exposures.

---

129   Out of 109 significant institutions directly supervised by the ECB as of mid-2023, 87 were headquartered in the euro area (the other 22 were subsidiaries or branches of non-euro-area banking groups, for which the concept of domestic home bias within the euro area is less relevant). Of the 87, 85 disclosed their sovereign exposures in the EBA's 2023 transparency exercise (the missing two, Austria's Addiko Bank and Lithuania's Siauliu Bankas, are very small). The measure of regulatory capital chosen in these calculations, known as Tier 1, is the one commonly used in regulations on banks' credit exposures.

130   In 2012, 97 percent of Greece's private-sector creditors took a nominal haircut of 53.5 percent (Gong, 2020).

131   Mid-2016 is taken as earlier point of reference as the data point analysed in the author's earlier in-depth study of sovereign exposures (Véron, 2017). It also represents the immediate aftermath of the euro-area crisis.

Table 1: Sovereign exposures of significant euro-area banks, mid-2023

Country	No. of banks	Total assets (€ms)	Sovereign exposures (€m)				Home bias				Capital coverage			
			Global	Euro area	Domestic	Median	Average	Country-wide	Median	Average	Country-wide	Median	Average	Country-wide
Austria	5	681,257	87,465	35,332	17,243	49%	59%	49%	36%	42%	33%			
Belgium	4	609,438	88,675	53,903	35,922	64%	67%	67%	60%	81%	104%			
Cyprus	2	44,959	2,889	2,424	1,964	82%	82%	81%	64%	64%	63%			
Estonia	2	21,763	1,766	1,732	395	36%	36%	23%	30%	30%	21%			
Finland	3	713,226	42,103	24,031	19,040	47%	57%	79%	18%	358%	45%			
France	9	8,782,425	1,049,032	707,550	532,011	87%	80%	75%	69%	449%	113%			
Germany	16	3,857,145	353,437	219,692	151,426	84%	75%	69%	82%	112%	80%			
Greece	4	303,394	51,846	47,838	32,867	67%	71%	69%	174%	157%	152%			
Ireland	2	266,214	12,494	10,811	8,333	77%	77%	77%	43%	43%	43%			
Italy	12	2,617,543	484,850	392,608	273,641	73%	73%	70%	187%	268%	164%			
Latvia	1	4,820	1,012	890	372	42%	42%	42%	95%	95%	95%			
Luxembourg	3	99,938	11,917	8,191	2,329	10%	23%	28%	27%	23%	33%			
Malta	2	19,163	3,438	3,138	1,384	23%	23%	44%	65%	65%	109%			
Netherlands	6	2,340,406	230,578	163,774	94,437	30%	45%	58%	18%	511%	71%			
Portugal	3	232,419	51,622	43,599	20,101	45%	46%	46%	103%	131%	114%			
Slovenia	2	30,691	4,547	2,227	955	51%	51%	43%	28%	28%	30%			
Spain	9	3,680,057	511,963	331,885	250,344	77%	76%	75%	207%	219%	123%			
Total	**85**	**24,304,858**	**2,989,633**	**2,049,623**	**1,442,764**	**71%**	**65%**	**70%**	**89%**	**206%**	**106%**			

Source: Bruegel, EBA; see Appendix A for underlying bank-level data. Home bias is defined as the ratio of domestic sovereign exposures to euro-area sovereign exposures. Capital coverage is defined as the ratio of domestic sovereign exposures to Tier 1 capital. Country-wide ratios are defined as the ratio of aggregates for all banks in the country sample. The ratios in the bottom line are calculated across all 85 banks in the sample without consideration of home country. Note: some countries (eg the Netherlands) show a large difference between average and median because of outliers, typically banks that are specialised in lending to local government.

Table 2: Sovereign exposures of a sample of significant euro-area banks, mid-2016 and mid-2023

Country	Number of banks	Mid-2016			Mid-2023		
		Assets (€ms)	Median home bias	Median capital coverage	Assets (€ms)	Median home bias	Median capital coverage
Austria	4	394,473	68%	86%	651,699	47%	32%
Belgium	4	523,214	62%	192%	609,438	64%	60%
Cyprus	2	29,770	92%	47%	44,959	82%	64%
Finland	2	426,006	29%	18%	664,849	36%	11%
France	7	7,484,142	76%	82%	8,342,970	77%	58%
Germany	13	4,061,947	85%	216%	3,692,147	81%	70%
Greece	4	308,668	72%	50%	303,394	67%	174%
Ireland	2	223,654	69%	71%	266,214	77%	43%
Italy	6	1,917,721	73%	184%	1,947,820	70%	128%
Malta	2	13,287	41%	122%	19,163	23%	65%
Netherlands	5	2,217,237	38%	62%	2,264,497	20%	14%
Portugal	3	227,713	84%	135%	232,419	45%	103%
Slovenia	1	11,761	78%	141%	24,701	40%	33%
Spain	3	2,296,838	78%	129%	2,745,146	77%	97%
Total	**58**	**20,136,432**	**77%**	**129%**	**21,809,415**	**69%**	**72%**

Source: Bruegel, EBA, SNL Financial (assets for the 2016 panel, measured at end-2015). Note: same definitions as Table 1. See Appendix A for underlying bank-level data.

The challenge posed by sovereign exposures, including their contribution to the bank-sovereign vicious circle, was diagnosed late in the sequence of discovery detailed in chapter 3. This may be because it was not identified as a problem by national supervisors, who consequently did not raise it as long as they were exclusively in charge, and also quite plainly because for a long time there was no data publicly available about it. The first systematic collection of data on euro-area banks' sovereign exposures appears to have occurred during the stress testing exercise led by the EBA shortly after its establishment. Results were published in July 2011, based on end-2010 data, "*after very controversial discussions*" within the EBA Board of Supervisors (ie among national bank supervisors) according to the EBA's leading officials at the time (Enria *et al*, 2016). The detailed disclosure format then allowed academics and analysts to observe sovereign exposures and home-bias patterns for the first time on the basis of reliable and comparable data, leading to a body of literature that only developed from then.

Early analyses tended to focus on cross-border financial contagion (eg Bolton and Jeanne, 2011), but soon also identified domestic sovereign exposures as a component of the bank-sovereign vicious circle that would need to be mitigated by specific policies. One of the first such recommendations read: "*Protecting the banking system from the sovereign requires a cap on exposures (single obligor limits) with respect to sovereign debtors, including the sovereign in the home country of a banking group*" (Zettelmeyer, 2011). Even so, concentrated domestic sovereign exposures do not appear to have featured prominently as a policy concern during the decision-making episode of 2012 as recounted in chapter 3.

The issue only started to become prominent when European banking supervision came into place. In February 2014, Danièle Nouy, newly appointed chair of the ECB Supervisory Board, mentioned the home bias as a concern, while acknowledging that it was too early to consider immediate action to address it[132]. One year later, the European Systemic Risk Board, an EU-wide macroprudential body hosted by the ECB, published a seminal report that included a detailed analysis of home bias in the sovereign exposures of euro-area banks (and insurers) and an exploration of policy options to address it (ESRB, 2015). These options were about replacing the existing framework, in which banks' sovereign exposures to EU countries were essentially exempted from any capital requirements, with regulatory constraints focused on either credit risk (specific disincentives against exposures to the sovereigns perceived as less creditworthy, eg those with high public debt or low credit ratings) or concentration risk (eg caps on a bank's exposure to a given sovereign, or higher capital requirements on concentrated exposures), or a combination of the two[133]. The second option – capital charges that rise progressively when the ratio of credit exposure to Tier-1 capital exceeds a certain threshold – is generally referred to in the RTSE debate as *"sovereign concentration charges"*[134].

On this solid early analytical basis, however, no policy consensus emerged on how to address the challenge of sovereign exposures, or even how to acknowledge it in public pronouncements. The deadlock and its interaction with the policy debate about crisis management and deposit insurance are further analysed later in this chapter.

---

132   Alice Ross, 'Let weak banks die, says eurozone super-regulator', *Financial Times*, 9 February 2014, https://www.ft.com/content/c27d19b4-917b-11e3-8fb3-00144feab7de.

133   In principle, supervisors can impose limits on banks' individual risk exposures under their discretionary (pillar 2) authority. Sovereign exposures, however, do not unambiguously fall under the micro-prudential mandate of European banking supervision, at least for countries with investment-grade credit ratings. Thus the need to address the home-bias challenge through generally applicable (pillar 1) regulation, specifically changes to the EU Capital Requirements Regulation.

134   The corresponding policy trade-offs, particularly about calibration and transitional arrangements, are discussed in detail in Véron (2017).

Crisis management and deposit insurance: legislation

As recounted in chapter 3, Europe entered the great financial crisis with a 'deep-pocket' approach to bank crisis management and resolution, under which national governments were expected to compensate the claimants of failed banks to ensure financial stability. Correlated with this general preference for state-directed rescues, deposit insurance has long been a marginal element of the banking policy framework in most European countries, unlike in the United States where the FDIC has been viewed since its creation in the 1930s as the main protagonist in bank crisis management. Three decades ago, Xavier Vives (1992) thus observed:

> "Deposit insurance has played a major role in providing stability to the USA financial system. Its role in Europe has been much more limited, being introduced in most countries in the late 1970s having more in mind small depositor's protection than financial stability. [...] A striking feature of deposit insurance in Europe is that it remains largely unknown to the public, at least up to now. This is probably because it is expected, consistently with experience on banks failures in several European countries, that banks in trouble will be bailed out by the government."

Things had not fundamentally changed by the time the financial crisis erupted in 2007-2008. The exception that proved the rule was Northern Rock in the UK, which experienced an old-fashioned bank run in September 2007 because of an ill-designed deposit-insurance scheme that did not entail full reimbursement even of small insured deposits, a mistake that was corrected soon afterwards.

At the peak of transatlantic financial dislocation in September and October 2008, Europeans were horrified by the US executive decision to let Lehman Brothers (technically a non-bank) fail. At a meeting of finance ministers of the Group of Seven countries on 10 October 2008, Europeans insisted that the published declaration should mention agreement to take "*decisive action and use all available tools to support systemically important financial institutions and prevent their failure*"[135]. The massive cost of bank rescues, combined with awareness of the vocal US debate about 'too-big-to-fail' banks, then led to a gradual realisation in some countries that a better sharing of such costs with private-sector creditors might be desirable.

But that was far from a universal view: other countries, influenced in no small part by considerations of banking nationalism, still maintained that full support for failing banks was the better option. The UK introduced a special resolution regime in its Banking Act of February 2009, intended to prevent a repeat of the RBS debacle, and Germany adopted a broadly similar Restructuring Act in December 2010, though in practice only applicable to its commercial banks and not to the two IPSs of public and cooperative banks. The European Commission proceeded cautiously, and undertook repeated rounds of communication and consultation in 2009, 2010 and 2011 before venturing a legislative proposal.

In the meantime, more than any Europe-wide political backlash against taxpayer generosity to bankers *per se*, it was the growing evidence of the bank-sovereign vicious circle that supported a common EU approach that would better protect national creditworthiness against the cost of bank rescues. In 2011 and early 2012, the imposition of losses on junior creditors of failing European banks became increasingly accepted practice, though primarily in cases where the sovereign itself

---

[135] G7 Finance Ministers and Central Bank Governors Plan of Action, 10 October 2008, Washington DC, available at https://elischolar.library.yale.edu/ypfs-documents/7354/.

was under financial stress (such as Ireland and Spain) and much less so in other countries[136]. Eventually, after years of consensus-building, the Commission published in early June 2012 its legislative proposal for a Bank Recovery and Resolution Directive (BRRD), which was largely inspired by the British legislation of 2009, and thus foresaw bail-in of creditors (ie forced losses) as a possible tool for authorities in charge of resolving a failing bank.

This was the fluid context in which the decision on direct recapitalisation of banks by the ESM was made and then largely unmade in summer 2012, as recounted in chapter 3. By September, as it appeared that the worst phase of market pressure was probably over, the finance ministers of the three countries most hostile to the direct recapitalisation idea – Germany's Schäuble and his Dutch and Finnish counterparts – issued a joint statement that placed yet more conditions on future consideration of ESM direct recapitalisation, which would make its implementation practically impossible[137].

---

136 For example, in early September 2012, the French authorities extended a full guarantee on all liabilities of Crédit Immobilier de France, a failing bank that was subsequently placed into orderly liquidation. In Ireland, the shift of political consensus in favour of "*burning the bondholders*" of failing banks was catalysed by the advice the country received from the International Monetary Fund during the negotiation of its assistance programme in late 2010 (Véron, 2016, page 18). Technically, most losses incurred by Irish bank creditors in 2011 were associated with voluntary restructurings, albeit under threat of mandatory bail-in.

137 Joint Statement of the Ministers of Finance of Finland, Germany and the Netherlands, 25 September 2012, https://www.eerstekamer.nl/eu/overig/20121001/gezamenlijke_verklaring_van_de/document. In line with that statement, the ESM adopted a guideline on direct recapitalisation in December 2014 that effectively precluded its future use, as demonstrated by the experience of ESM-led simulation exercises (see ESM, 2019, pages 297-298) and the fact that it was indeed never triggered in subsequent years. The specific case of Ireland, which held a claim on ESM direct recapitalisation from the euro-area summit statement of 29 June 2012, was settled by a favourable transaction involving promissory notes that was executed in early 2013 (Véron, 2016, page 19). A French-German declaration in June 2018 advocated the eventual termination of the ESM direct recapitalisation instrument, which was endorsed at a December 2018 euro-area summit.

As a substitute for direct recapitalisation, the European Council of 13-14 December 2012 decided that the BRRD resolution framework proposed in June by the European Commission would be managed in the euro area in a coordinated manner, and called for a *"single resolution mechanism"* (SRM), the name of which echoed the single supervisory mechanism of European banking supervision. In March 2013, following turbulent handling of the crisis in Cyprus, Eurogroup president Jeroen Dijsselbloem stated that *"We should aim at a situation where we will never need to even consider direct* [ESM] *recap*[italisation of banks]"[138]. The official rhetoric correspondingly shifted in 2013 towards emphasis on 'private-sector risk-sharing', namely that the SRM would allow failing banks to be closed without recourse to public money, thus attempting to bury both the previous year's concept of ESM direct recapitalisation and, more generally, the deep-pocket approach to banking crises that had been generally adopted in Europe for decades until the early 2010s.

Even so, finding consensus on what the called-for single resolution mechanism would actually mean in practice turned out to be difficult and painful. After much wrangling, the European Commission proposed on 10 July 2013 a legislative text for the SRM Regulation. That text foresaw the establishment of a new EU agency in Brussels, the Single Resolution Board (SRB), at the centre of a new euro-area resolution framework that would also include a Single Resolution Fund (SRF) managed by the SRB. One of many controversial features of the Commission's proposal was its choice of Article 114 TFEU, the treaty basis for the EU's body of internal (single) market legislation, as the legal basis for the SRM. This raised at least three main concerns. First, the SRB's primary objective was to support financial stability, which is not necessarily aligned with internal market

---

138 Peter Spiegel, 'Cyprus rescue signals new line on bailouts', *Financial Times*, 25 March 2013, https://www.ft.com/content/68c9c18e-955e-11e2-a151-00144feabdc0.

integration. Second, the SRB would only have jurisdiction over countries of the euro area and those that join the banking union voluntarily, thus not covering the entire internal market. Third, there were objections to Article 114 as a basis for enabling the SRB to raise levies from banks to build up the SRF. The latter were eventually addressed by creating an alternative legal base through an *ad-hoc* inter-governmental agreement.

The acrimonious SRM negotiation extended throughout 2013. Unlike the previous year's sequence on banking supervision, it did not involve directly the political principals (heads of state and government), but was led by finance ministers, with little pressure from financial markets. Nevertheless, there was still enough of a shared sentiment of crisis that even the most reluctant countries could not veto everything (Nielsen and Smeets, page 1250). There was also a strong common political objective of finding a compromise before the end of the EU legislative term in the spring of 2014. The German negotiators long insisted that resolution decisions should be made directly by the EU Council, a stance that one of them described with hindsight in 2015 as *"pretty much nonsense"* because *"it complicates the procedure to an extent which is questionable […] but it is a question of priorities, and our priority was attaching strings to the mechanism"* (Schäfer, 2017, page 199). Germany ended up renouncing that stance and accepting the outlines of the legal construct that the European Commission had proposed in July 2013[139]. Possibly as an offset, it secured the exemption of most smaller banks from the scope of direct SRB authority in case of failure, in contrast to the more integrated framework (albeit with delegation of day-to-day tasks to national authorities) in the SSM

---

[139] Alex Barker, Peter Spiegel and Stefan Wagstyl, 'Berlin gives ground in banking union debate', *Financial Times*, 6 December 2013, https://www.ft.com/content/0ba3d460-5e97-11e3-8621-00144feabdc0. Even after the SRM Regulation's enactment in 2014, this construct has elicited lingering scepticism among some legal scholars; see for example Tuominen (2017).

Regulation (Howarth and Quaglia, 2014)[140].

With these compromises, the SRM Regulation was eventually agreed by the EU Council in December 2013, complemented with a political declaration that a *"common backstop"* would be provided to support the financial firepower of the SRF and "will be fully operational at the latest after ten years", meaning by December 2023[141]. The BRRD and SRM Regulation were subsequently finalised by the European Parliament and Council, in parallel with an intergovernmental agreement on how banks in the different countries would contribute to the SRF, albeit with multiple national compartments that would only be fully mutualised (ie the SRF would become a truly single fund) after an initial build-up period of ten years[142]. The full package of texts was enacted in the spring and early summer of 2014[143].

That sequence of decision-making did not include any consideration of integrating deposit insurance at euro-area level because, as mentioned

---

140   The SRB has authority to include some more banks within its scope than those designated as significant by European banking supervision, but there have been only a few additions in practice. In addition, the SRB may intervene in resolution action undertaken on failing small banks by national resolution authorities. There have been no such actions to date, however, despite the fact that 68 less-significant institutions (with aggregate assets of about €700 billion) were described by the SRB as *"earmarked for resolution"* as of 2023 (SRB, 2023, page 15).

141   'Statement of Eurogroup and ECOFIN Ministers on the SRM backstop', 18 December 2013, https://www.consilium.europa.eu/media/21899/20131218-srm-backstop-statement.pdf. As will be noted below, the ten-year deadline for establishing the backstop has not been met.

142   In line with that agreement, the SRF became fully mutualised on 31 December 2023. The transitory national compartments have thus ceased to exist, as have the national loan facility agreements that supported them. See SRB press release of 15 February 2024, 'Single Resolution Fund: no expected contribution in 2024 as target level reached', https://www.srb.europa.eu/en/content/single-resolution-fund-no-expected-contribution-2024-target-level-reached.

143   BRRD 2014/59/EU of 15 May 2014; SRM Regulation (EU) 806/2014 of 15 July 2014; and Inter-Governmental Agreement on contributions to the SRF finalised in mid-May 2014 and ratified by all participating countries by December 2015, https://data.consilium.europa.eu/doc/document/ST 8457 2014 INIT/EN/pdf (Schäfer, 2017, page 4).

in chapter 3, the principal players in June 2012 had made a conscious decision to leave it for a later stage – despite its advocacy by EU institutions and the IMF, and its fleeting mention in the G20 declaration at Los Cabos a few days earlier (see footnote 62). A directive on partial harmonisation of deposit guarantee schemes was also adopted in 2014[144], but left deposit insurance firmly anchored at national level and thus still as a potential contributor to the bank-sovereign vicious circle. The responsible European Commissioner, Michel Barnier, had tried to reintroduce a European deposit insurance project in the late summer of 2012, but had to backtrack swiftly in the face of immediate and uncompromising German pushback[145]. A compendium of relevant European Council conclusions on banking union, published at the end of the EU parliamentary term in mid-2014, does not include a single reference to, let alone endorsement of, a European deposit insurance mechanism (Council of the EU, 2014). Even the ECB, while being consistently clear about the need in principle for a European deposit insurance scheme to support a resilient banking union, conceded during that period that it would only be considered *"at a later stage"* (eg Coeuré, 2013).

In comparison with the package enacted in 2014, legislation adopted since then in the area of bank crisis management, resolution and deposit insurance has been of minor consequence from a banking union standpoint and is not detailed here. Legislative initiatives that have been proposed but not adopted yet are described later in this chapter.

---

144   Deposit Guarantee Scheme Directive 2014/49/EU of 16 April 2014.
145   Alex Barker, 'Brussels shelved bank deposit scheme', *Financial Times*, 13 September 2012, https://www.ft.com/content/e2dd12ec-fdbe-11e1-9901-00144feabdc0.

Crisis management practice and comparison with the United States

The practical implementation of the BRRD-SRM legislation of 2014 so far has presented a mixed picture. For simplicity, cases of crisis management and resolution until the end of 2015 are left aside, because the 2014 package only became fully applicable on 1 January 2016. With these parameters in mind, the first eight years of implementation of the BRRD-SRM framework in the euro area stand in some contrast to the overall success of European banking supervision as assessed in the previous chapter.

On the positive side, the SRB has developed into an increasingly established organisation. It has imposed increasingly significant requirements on the banks within its scope to raise debt instruments presumed to be 'bail-inable' (meaning that in a resolution scenario, the holders of those instruments can incur losses, ie be bailed in, without generating systemic instability). The SRB has also engaged in international cooperation, particularly in the form of regular crisis simulation exercises with its major counterparts in the United Kingdom and the United States[146].

The first real test of the SRB's crisis management capability was the resolution of Banco Popular Español in June 2017, which was passed with qualified success. After that Spanish bank was declared 'failing or likely to fail' by the ECB on 6 June, the resolution process led by the SRB in liaison with the Spanish authorities was orderly. The SRB's resolution scheme for Banco Popular was subsequently the target of multiple lawsuits (around a hundred legal cases over half a decade). The SRB was vindicated when the Court of Justice of the EU dismissed all cases in their

---

146 See for example FDIC press release of 16 April 2024, 'Principals of U.S., European Banking Union, and U.K. Financial Authorities Meet for Regular Coordination Exercise on Cross-Border Resolution Planning', https://www.fdic.gov/news/press-releases/principals-us-european-banking-union-and-uk-financial-authorities-meet-regular.

entirety in a ruling on 1 June 2022[147], even though cases are still ongoing in other jurisdictions.

Banco Popular Español and subsequent cases have demonstrated that the SRB is able to take rapid action in at least some situations, despite multiple concerns expressed early on about the complexity of its formal decision-making procedures resulting from the convoluted compromises made in 2013 during the negotiation of the SRM Regulation[148]. Until now, Banco Popular Español remains by far the largest European bank to have been closed via the BRRD resolution process in an orderly manner and with no recourse to public money[149]. Less exemplarily, the early phases of the process that led to the resolution of Banco Popular Español were marred by serious communication issues that appeared to involve the SRB and its consultations with national authorities[150].

Despite the reassuring aspects of the Banco Popular Español case, however, a consensus has formed in the late 2010s that the SRM has generally

---

147 Court of Justice of the EU press release of 1 June 2022, 'The actions seeking annulment of the resolution scheme in respect of Banco Popular and/or the Commission decision endorsing that scheme are dismissed in their entirety', https://curia.europa.eu/jcms/upload/docs/application/pdf/2022-06/cp220090en.pdf.

148 Sven Giegold, 'Single Resolution Board commits to report about obstacles to resolution in national and EU legislation', sven-giegold.de, 29 January 2016, https://sven-giegold.de/single-resolution-board-commits-to-report-about-obstacles-to-resolution-in-national-and-eu-legislation/.

149 SRB Chair Elke König commented that the euro area had been *"lucky"* that several features of the Banco Popular Español case made resolution comparatively easy. See Jim Brunsden, 'Tighter EU curbs urged on winding down banks', *Financial Times*, 8 August 2017, https://www.ft.com/content/545c1790-7b7f-11e7-ab01-a13271d1ee9c. Credit Suisse, in March 2023, was not closed through a resolution process, which was considered but eventually not triggered. Instead, it was acquired by its peer UBS via a transaction facilitated by the Swiss authorities.

150 See *Bloomberg* Markets TV interview with SRB Chair Elke König, 'Single Resolution Says EU Shouldn't Be Bailing Out Banks', 23 May 2017, https://www.bloomberg.com/news/videos/2017-05-23/single-resolution-eu-shouldn-t-be-bailing-banks-video; Francesco Guarascio, 'EU warned of wind-down risk for Spain's Banco Popular – source', Reuters, 31 May 2017, https://www.reuters.com/article/uk-banco-popular-m-a-eu-idUKKBN18R25M/; Eva

not worked as intended (eg Tröger, 2017; Restoy *et al*, 2020). To a significant extent, this is linked to a feature of BRRD that gives the resolution authority (eg the SRB), once a bank has been found failing or likely to fail, the power to determine whether the use of the resolution process under EU law set out by BRRD would be in the public interest. If that public interest assessment is positive, then the resolution authority takes the lead in the resolution procedure, as the SRB did with Banco Popular Español. If the assessment is negative, the national authorities apply normal insolvency proceedings under national law, even in the case of large banks within the scope of authority of the SRB. That division of tasks has created many challenges that may not have been fully understood at the time the legislation was agreed (Tröger and Kotovskaia, 2022).

Back in 2014, most lawmakers involved in drafting the BRRD envisioned the resolution process it introduced as the 'new normal' for banks that would be found unviable, except the very smallest, for which the alternative route of normal insolvency proceedings might be followed[151]. Aside from Banco Popular Español, however, the practice

---

Díaz, 'El juez del Popular cita a la presidenta del JUR para que explique las filtraciones a la prensa,' *El Economista*, 19 May 2021, https://www.eleconomista.es/empresas-finanzas/noticias/11224677/05/21/El-juez-del-Popular-cita-a-la-presidenta-del-JUR-para-que-explique-las-filtraciones-a-la-prensa.html.

151 The text of the BRRD itself, which resulted from multiple compromises among numerous negotiators, suggests that its resolution process should not be ruled out for any bank no matter how small, but does not provide full clarity. Recital 29 of BRRD states: "*Due to the potentially systemic nature of all* [credit] *institutions, it is crucial, in order to maintain financial stability, that authorities have the possibility to resolve any institution.*" Recital 45 states: "*A failing institution should in principle be liquidated under normal insolvency proceedings. However, liquidation under normal insolvency proceedings might jeopardise financial stability, interrupt the provision of critical functions, and affect the protection of depositors. In such a case it is highly likely that there would be a public interest in placing the institution under resolution and applying resolution tools rather than resorting to normal insolvency proceedings.*" Recital 46 adds: "*The winding up of a failing institution through normal insolvency proceedings should always be considered before resolution tools are applied.*"

has not been generally in line with that expectation. No small bank in the euro area has been resolved using the BRRD process (ie following a positive public-interest assessment by the national resolution authority after having been determined failing or likely to fail), in contrast to the practice of several national authorities in EU non-euro-area countries. Even for larger banks, resolution has been the exception rather than the rule. In the early twin cases of Banca Popolare di Vicenza and Veneto Banca, two mid-sized banks in the same Italian region of Venetia that the ECB simultaneously determined as failing or likely to fail in June 2017, the SRB made a negative public interest assessment, allowing the two banks to be handled through a resolution-like process under Italian national law (*liquidazione coatta amministrativa*) that entailed the provision of large public subsidies to avoid loss-bearing by creditors[152]. Other cases that were widely viewed as problematic involved struggling banks receiving fresh capital from government entities and thus avoiding being deemed failing or likely to fail. Examples include Italy's Monte dei Paschi di Siena and Germany's HSH Nordbank and Nord/LB[153]. In the cases of HSH Nordbank, the two Venetian banks and Monte dei Paschi, state aid was granted on the basis of debatable assessments of risks to financial stability, had these banks' creditors incurred losses.

---

152 Berg and Lind (2023) made an acerbic reference to national liquidation procedures (ie normal insolvency proceedings in the language of BRRD) as "*often another term for bail out.*" In the case of the two Venetian banks, the subsidies were authorised by the European Commission as liquidation aid. While none of this was technically in breach of BRRD, it does not appear that most BRRD legislators in 2012-2014 considered that a failing bank case under national insolvency proceedings might be granted state aid.

153 Again, none of these cases represented an unambiguous breach of the BRRD. For Monte dei Paschi, the Italian state implemented a precautionary recapitalisation, which is allowed by the BRRD under a number of conditions, which were deemed to have been met and not subsequently challenged. The European Commission, in its competition policy enforcement capacity, authorised the state aid in the cases of Monte dei Paschi and HSH Nordbank, and determined that the Nord/LB public recapitalisation was made on non-preferential terms and therefore did not constitute state aid.

For a few years, the SRB appeared to rationalise its choice of negative public interest assessments, in cases such as the two Venetian banks, by maintaining that *"resolution is for the few* [ie the very largest banks], *not for the many"*[154]. In 2021, however, it appeared to pivot away from that stance and to signal a broader scope for positive public interest assessments in the future[155]. In early 2022, the SRB sent further confusing signals with the resolution of Sberbank Europe in the immediate aftermath of Russia's invasion of Ukraine. Sberbank Europe's resolution was orderly but highlighted the hard-to-predict nature of the SRB's public interest assessments[156].

Other authorities, outside the euro area but within the EU, have implemented the same BRRD legislation differently. In Denmark, the national resolution authority has established a record of positive public interest assessments even for very small banks, resulting in their resolution under EU rather than national law with no special protection for uninsured

---

154 See for example SRB (2019) and Elke König, 'Completing the crisis management framework: a centralized administrative liquidation tool for banks', *Views The Eurofi Magazine*, 24 April 2020, https://www.srb.europa.eu/en/content/eurofi-article-elke-konig-centralized-administrative-liquidation-tool-banks-zagreb-april.

155 An SRB document of May 2021 stated: *"The current expectation (in resolution planning) is that nearly all banks under SRB direct remit will have a positive PIA"* (public interest assessment). SRB, 'A blueprint for the CMDI framework review', 18 May 2021, https://www.srb.europa.eu/system/files/media/document/2021-05-18_srb_views_on_cmdi_1.pdf.

156 The SRB's prior resolution plan for Sberbank Europe AG, a fully-owned subsidiary of Sberbank of Russia, had implied a positive public interest assessment. But after both the ECB and SRB had determined it to be failing or likely to fail, the SRB made a negative public interest assessment for Sberbank Europe AG, resulting in its liquidation under Austrian law. The SRB simultaneously made a positive assessment, followed by resolution decisions, for Sberbank Europe's smaller subsidiaries in Croatia and Slovenia, both of which were taken over by local peers. See SRB press release of 1 March 2022, 'Sberbank Europe AG: Croatian and Slovenian subsidiaries resume operations after being sold while no resolution action is required for Austrian parent company', https://www.srb.europa.eu/en/content/sberbank-europe-ag-croatian-and-slovenian-subsidiaries-resume-operations-after-being-sold; and Magnus *et al* (2022).

depositors. The Danish authorities insist that this stance can also be sustained in the future for larger banks, because of clear understanding by the Danish public of what is protected and what is not (Danmarks Nationalbank, 2021)[157]. The SRB has acknowledged the difference between its stance and that of Denmark (PIIE, 2023). It remains to be seen whether the SRB can make its stance on public interest assessments more predictable within the constraints and incentives of the current legislative framework, and the way the European Commission implements its state-aid control mandate in the banking sector.

Here too, a comparison with the United States is worth attempting. Contrary to what was observed about supervision, the US crisis management and resolution framework is considerably more streamlined and predictable than its equivalent(s) in the euro area (even though the events of March 2023 placed it under an unflattering spotlight). The US framework also embeds a high degree of market discipline, sustaining the comparison with the above-described Danish practice: in one fifth of the bank failures during the three decades from 1992 to 2022 (165 out of 838 failures), uninsured depositors incurred losses, even though most of the banks for which this happened were small and, as a consequence, the aggregate loss from all these cases, at $285 million, was not very large (FDIC, 2023, page 22).

There is only one avenue for dealing with failing US banks: resolution by the FDIC, without anything in the US framework that would resemble the public interest assessment introduced by the BRRD. The

---

157 Strict bail-in was applied in the respective failures of Amagerbanken and Fjordbank Mors, which were handled in 2011 and thus predated the BRRD and its transposition into Danish law. Two other Danish banks, Andelskassen JAK Slagelse and Københavns Andelskasse, were similarly resolved in 2015 and 2018 respectively under the BRRD resolution framework. Both were extremely small (adding up to less than €100 million in total assets) and marred by allegations of fraud and/or money laundering, which complicates the assessment of the financial stability implications of uninsured depositors incurring losses.

FDIC is the only agency in charge for banks[158], and the National Credit Union Administration for credit unions. By contrast, in the euro area, multiple complementary and overlapping mandates involve the SRB, the European Commission (as a participant in the resolution process), national resolution authorities (which play a role even in an SRB-directed resolution process of a significant institution), national deposit-guarantee schemes (which in many countries are separate from the national resolution authority – and Austria, Germany and Italy each have more than one national deposit guarantee system), and the courts that are involved in many national insolvency proceedings. In addition, the EU Council is involved in some aspects of resolution decision-making, as is the European Commission in line with its mandate of state-aid control if any use of public money is involved[159].

The complexity associated with the involvement of so many parties generates uncertainty and countless opportunities for dysfunction (Tröger, 2017; Gelpern and Véron, 2019). Managing and resolving a banking crisis is generally a thankless task. The contrast between the US framework, where that responsibility is unambiguously assigned to one organisation, and the euro area, where it is scattered across many, only highlights the flaws of the European framework. Specifically, the public interest assessment functions in practice as an *"allocator of resolution cases"* with powerful incentives for SRB board members *"to brush conflicted cases*

---

158 In addition, the FDIC has so-called orderly liquidation authority to resolve non-banks, including bank holding companies, that are determined to be systemically important. This process, established by the Dodd-Frank Act of 2010 and so far never triggered, entails coordination with the US Treasury and the Federal Reserve (FDIC, 2024).

159 Two separate arms of the European Commission may thus be involved: the directorate-general in charge of financial services participates directly in the decision-making on euro-area-level bank resolution, and has set up a permanent dedicated Resolution Task Force for that purpose; and the directorate-general in charge of competition policy carries out state-aid control.

aside if they indeed wish to avoid conflict with national representatives and stakeholders" (Tröger and Kotovskaia, 2022, page 12).

The transatlantic difference in financial resources, by contrast, is less significant than sometimes portrayed. After a decade of build-up, the SRF reached its target level of €78 billion by end-2023. An additional €50 billion of financial means was stored in the banking union countries' 25 deposit guarantee schemes as of end-2022 (though the latter, obviously, are not mutualised)[160]. By end-2023, the FDIC's Deposit Insurance Fund reached $122 billion and the National Credit Union Administration's Share Insurance Fund had an additional $21 billion[161]. The FDIC has additional capacity to borrow, but that is quantitatively limited and the FDIC has been reluctant to use it historically[162]. The challenge of the SRB's financial firepower is real, and further detailed below, but that problem is not nearly as fundamental as those associated with ambiguous assignment of authority.

The contrast between the banking union's shaky resolution framework and the strength of European banking supervision is in part a consequence of the sequence of policymaking. Negotiations on the SSM Regulation mostly took place in the second half of 2012, when the general atmosphere was still of high uncertainty and elevated danger of euro-area break-up. Negotiations on the SRM Regulation, meanwhile, extended throughout 2013, with a lesser sense of vital emergency. The discussion on supervision involved the heads of state and government, while that on resolution was overwhelmingly left to finance ministers. The scope for consistent radical reform was thus greater for the SSM than for the SRM Regulation.

---

160   Calculated by the author from SRB and EBA disclosures.
161   Based on FDIC and National Credit Union Association disclosures.
162   The FDIC did borrow from the US Treasury in the early 1990s but decided not to do so during the Great Financial Crisis, despite a negative accounting balance of its Deposit Insurance Fund (DIF) from late 2009 to early 2011. Throughout that period, the DIF maintained positive portfolio liquidity by raising an additional deposit insurance levy (*"special assessment"* in FDIC parlance) from the US banking sector (FDIC, 2017, pages 156-161).

Negotiations without end: the nexus of sovereign exposures, crisis management and deposit insurance

Following European Parliament elections in May 2014, former Luxembourg prime minister Jean-Claude Juncker was chosen to lead the new European Commission. In his maiden policy speech, he committed to be *"active and vigilant in ensuring that we implement the new supervisory and resolution rules fully"* without any indication of follow-up legislative projects, while simultaneously trumpeting a separate initiative dubbed the Capital Markets Union, which is left outside the scope of this book (Juncker, 2014). After the hurdle of the comprehensive assessment was passed and the ECB began its new role as supervisor in November 2014, discussions soon restarted on completing the work that had been so momentously initiated in the previous EU legislative term. In March 2015, the ESRB issued its already-mentioned report on the challenge of concentrated sovereign exposures, thus placing that issue on the agenda for legislative reform. Soon afterwards, the European Economic and Financial Committee (an advisory formation of the EU Council) created a high-level working group on RTSE, chaired by Danish central banker Per Callesen.

Meanwhile, Juncker took the lead in the preparation of a document labelled the 'Five Presidents' Report' in direct reference to Van Rompuy's Four Presidents' Report of June 2012, which had played such a pivotal role in the decision-making sequence that led to European banking supervision and subsequently to the Single Resolution Mechanism[163]. The new report, published in June 2015, singled out the *"urgency"* of creating a *"third pillar of a fully-fledged Banking Union alongside bank supervision and resolution"* and proposed the initiation of a European Deposit Insurance

---

163 Unlike in 2012, the president of the European Parliament was included in the list in addition to those of the European Commission, ECB, European Council, and Eurogroup, thus the increase from four to five presidents.

Scheme (EDIS) to that effect (Juncker, 2015). The European Commission subsequently published a legislative proposal for EDIS in November 2015, with a target date set (at the time) at mid-2024 for full mutualisation of the proposed system[164].

The Juncker Commission's EDIS proposal of November 2015, however, turned out to have been based on a mistaken assessment of the political dynamics at the time, even though it certainly responded to the desires of some member states. The Commission had published its BRRD proposal in June 2012 after repeated rounds of consultations over three years. It had unveiled its proposals for the SSM and SRM Regulations, respectively in September 2012 and July 2013, as matters of urgent consideration in crisis circumstances. In the case of EDIS, the Commission did not build a consensus ahead of publishing its proposal, nor were the circumstances dire enough to force rapid adoption. A few weeks earlier, in September 2015, the German authorities had circulated a document that ended with the terse phrase: "*To now start a discussion on further mutualization of bank risks through a common deposit insurance or an European deposit reinsurance scheme is unacceptable*"[165]. Shortly after the Commission published its EDIS proposal, the German Federal Finance Ministry's chief economist published a scornful critique, while protesting that his objections were "*not primarily a question of Germany's interests*"[166].

In January 2016, the EU Council established an "*ad hoc working*

---

164 See European Commission, 'Commission proposal for a European deposit insurance scheme (EDIS), 24 November 2015, https://finance.ec.europa.eu/publications/commission-proposal-european-deposit-insurance-scheme-edis_en.

165 German non-paper, 'The EMU needs a stronger Banking Union, but must get it right', 8 September 2015, https://blogs.ft.com/brusselsblog/files/2015/09/Nonpaperfinal_20150910091345.pdf.

166 Ludger Schuknecht, 'An insurance scheme that only ensures problems', *Frankfurter Allgemeine Zeitung*, 8 February 2016, https://blogs.faz.net/fazit/2016/02/08/an-insurance-scheme-that-only-ensures-problems-7298/.

party on the strengthening of the banking union" with an emphasis on the technical aspects of European deposit insurance. In spring 2016, the RTSE group chaired by Callesen delivered its report, but none of its output was made public, likely reflecting heightened sensitivities about the issue (Véron, 2017). A subsequent EU Council meeting in mid-June 2016 stated that any decision on sovereign exposures would be delayed until after the production of a report by the Basel Committee[167], a transparently dilatory approach since, as highlighted above, the home bias challenge is specific to monetary unions (of which the euro area is by far the largest) and can thus not be expected to be resolved by coordination at the global level[168]. The separate EDIS-centred working party would meet no fewer than forty-three times up to mid-2021, as documented in progress reports published by the successive rotating presidencies of the EU Council[169].

These documents give a sense of the deadlock that rapidly set in on both EDIS and RTSE, with numbingly repetitive arguments made by EU countries in successive discussion cycles. One of them characteristically noted, with reference to a meeting on RTSE in October 2020: "*Member States expressed well-known divergent views on capital charges*". The head of ECB banking supervision, Andrea Enria, later referred to the

---

167 Council document 10324/16, 17 June 2016.
168 The Basel Committee's report, published in December 2017, predictably stopped well short of providing solutions to the euro area's specific challenge (BCBS, 2017).
169 Council documents 10036/16 (14 June 2016); 14841/16 (25 November 2016); 9484/1/17 (12 June 2017); 14808/17 (24 November 2017); 9819/18 (12 June 2018); 14452/18 (23 November 2018); 9729/19 (4 June 2019); 14354/19 (25 November 2019); 8335/20 (29 May 2020); 13091/20 (23 November 2020); 9311/21 (2 June 2021); and 13965/21 (25 November 2021). Searchable by reference at https://www.consilium.europa.eu/en/documents-publications/public-register/public-register-search/.

discussions as *"totally mired in a cobweb of red lines by member states"*[170]. In addition to the call for a global agreement on RTSE within the Basel Committee, other delaying tactics included the claim that a loosely defined 'risk reduction' should be a preliminary condition for any consideration of risk sharing – in ostensible denial of the massive cross-border risk spillovers that had characterised the climax of euro-area crisis in 2011-2012.

This long period of stasis was punctuated by several attempts to forge at least a partial compromise, which however resolved nothing, but rather added to the general sense of despondency about completing the banking union. In October 2017, the European Commission (2017c) proposed a watered-down version of its EDIS concept. About a year later, the Austrian government, which held the rotating, six-month presidency of the EU Council proposed a *"hybrid model"* for European deposit insurance which further diluted the central component while retaining more prominence for existing national deposit guarantee schemes[171]. None of these got much traction, not least because the nature of deposit insurance must be clearly explainable to the general public in a situation of emergency. Obfuscation about where the ultimate responsibility resides therefore defeats the very purpose of the instrument. From that standpoint, leaving deposit insurance entirely at national level, as is currently the case, is arguably preferable to a complex halfway house that mixes European and national components. Any transition to an integrated system would inevitably entail some such complexity, but

---

170 Laura Noonan and Martin Arnold, 'Europe's top banking supervisor says fragmenting market raises risks', *Financial Times*, 30 October 2023, https://www.ft.com/content/a8d19b-fc-9ce3-432b-baa5-f749f3f23ddd.

171 Council document 14452/18, 23 November 2018.

should be kept as short as practically possible[172].

During the same period, policy attention was also devoted to the challenge known as 'liquidity in resolution', namely the probable need for public liquidity support in the period immediately following the resolution of a bank, until market participants regain trust that the bank is viable and can be funded under normal conditions. In other jurisdictions that have implemented the bail-in principle, such liquidity in resolution is typically provided by the central bank with a specific guarantee from the fiscal authorities[173]. In the euro area, it was put under the spotlight by the case of Banco Popular Español, even though the latter's acquisition by Santander conveniently sidestepped the need for additional public funding. No agreement was found on a fiscal guarantee to support liquidity in resolution, however, and the ECB argued that its mandate did not allow it to assume the corresponding risk on its own (Mersch, 2018). The five-year European term under Commission President Juncker ended with the adoption of several updates to the legislative package of 2013-2014[174], but no tangible progress on either EDIS or RTSE.

In July 2019, Ursula von der Leyen was chosen to succeed Juncker. In

---

172 In 2011-2012, the author introduced the idea of 'deposit reinsurance', where a European fund would back national deposit guarantee schemes (Véron, 2012), only intended as an explicitly temporary measure in the context of emergency, which should be rapidly replaced by a permanent integrated system where the authority resides squarely at the European level. The cascade of loss-taking 'compartments' in the deposit-insurance architecture sketched by Schnabel and Véron (2018) would be permanent, but entirely integrated at the European level in terms of governance and decision-making with no residual role for national authorities.

173 See for example the Bank of England's approach to resolution, also known as the 'Purple Book', first published in 2013 and updated in 2017 and 2023; https://www.bankofengland.co.uk/paper/2023/the-bank-of-englands-approach-to-resolution.

174 Acts known colloquially as CRR2 (Regulation (EU) 2019/876), SRMR2 (Regulation (EU) 2019/877), CRD5 (Directive (EU) 2019/878), BRRD2 (Directive (EU) 2019/879) of 20 May 2019.

her policy statement as president-elect of the European Commission, she committed to *"focus on completing the Banking Union"* and listed *"a common backstop to the Single Resolution Fund"* and *"a European Deposit Insurance Scheme"* as *"the missing elements of the Banking Union"*. She added: *"I will also put forward measures for a robust bank resolution and insolvency framework"* (von der Leyen, 2019). The ad-hoc working party on the strengthening of the banking union continued its seemingly endless negotiations, including throughout the disruption caused by the COVID-19 pandemic in 2020-2021. Much of the work focused on the highly complex cluster of reform themes around crisis management and deposit insurance. It had become increasingly clear, first, that (as noted above) the resolution framework introduced in 2014 was not working as intended, and second, that keeping the discussion on deposit insurance separate from that on resolution was counter-productive in terms of crisis management efficiency[175]. Increasingly, policymakers started referring to a *"European FDIC"* or otherwise highlighted the FDIC as the model to follow, although with various and sometimes mutually incompatible understandings of what that would mean in practice (Constâncio, 2018; Restoy, 2019; Majnoni D'Intignano et al, 2020)[176].

---

175 In addition to previously cited references, Taos (2021) presented a concise argument in favour of integrating resolution and deposit insurance.

176 See also Olaf Scholz, 'Germany will consider EU-wide bank deposit reinsurance', *Financial Times*, 5 November 2019, https://www.ft.com/content/82624c98-ff14-11e9-a530-16c6c29e-70ca. The idea of a European FDIC had been formulated by several observers in the early banking union debates of 2011-2013 (see for example Constâncio (2011) and Sheila Bair, 'It's time for a European FDIC', *Fortune*, 20 March 2013, https://fortune.com/2013/03/20/sheila-bair-its-time-for-a-european-fdic/). Rehn (2020, page 206) described a G7 meeting in May 2013 when *"Mario Draghi maintained that why we don't [sic] take directly the US FDIC law as the starting point* [for the SRM Regulation], *as we'd need uniform rules of the game."* With the finalisation of the SRM Regulation, direct reference to the FDIC as a model for the banking union then largely disappeared for half a decade, until it was revived by the ECB Vice President Vitor Constâncio in 2018 and then used by a number of other policymakers.

In 2021 and early 2022, prompted by Eurogroup President Paschal Donohoe, the outline of a compromise appeared to emerge, bringing together the debates on RTSE and EDIS. A draft Eurogroup statement leaked in April 2022 suggested in the medium term the gradual introduction of *"non-[credit-]risk weighted concentration charges for very high concentrations of sovereign holdings in banks' balance sheets"*[177]. This indicated a narrowing down of RTSE options compared with previous discussions, avoiding the procyclicality inherent in any approach that would penalise exposures to sovereigns deemed less creditworthy under an inevitably judgmental risk assessment, eg credit ratings, whereas sovereign concentration charges are inherently acyclical and avoid placing euro-area banks at a competitive disadvantage to their non-euro-area peers (Véron, 2017).

The draft statement also called for *"a common European deposit insurance fund, managed by the Single Resolution Board"*, and suggested that, also in the medium term, the *"Single Resolution Board assumes responsibility for the administration of the least-cost test for the possible use of EDIS and of DGS* [deposit guarantee scheme] *funds beyond payout"*, indicating an integration of resolution and deposit insurance. The document further suggested to gradually:

> *"introduce a reinsurance function by the European fund for national DGS funds: the European deposit insurance fund will gradually take over risks relating to depositors protection in the Banking Union and cover losses arising from the protection of depositors and financing of the resolution of credit institutions. The SRB may*

---

[177] Bjarke Smith-Meyer and Paola Tamma, 'Eurogroup chief eyes banking union breakthrough by 2024', *Politico Pro*, 26 April 2022, https://pro.politico.eu/news/eurogroup-chief-eyes-banking-union-breakthrough-by-2024. The document itself is available at https://aeur.eu/f/1G6.

authorise the use of the European deposit insurance fund to support measures beyond payout under the least-cost test. For its reinsurance function, the European deposit insurance fund is replenished jointly through the recovery from insolvency proceedings and through contributions from the financial industry in the Banking Union."

While this design stopped short of full integration of existing national deposit guarantee schemes into the European deposit insurance structure, it came close to that by granting ultimate authority to the SRB.

The leaking of that draft document, however, turned out not to be an indication of imminent agreement. On the contrary, the protracted negotiation process that had been initiated in early 2016 ended in apparent impasse less than two months later, in the runup to a Eurogroup meeting on 16 June 2022 when it appears that Italian refusal to consider any option for RTSE led to a complete breakdown of the discussion[178]. Unlike the draft that leaked in April, the Eurogroup statement made no mention of either RTSE or European deposit insurance, but only a noncommittal observation that the Eurogroup had *"explored ways to […] encourage greater diversification of banks' sovereign bond holdings in the EU,"* and a reference to deposit insurance exclusively in the context of improving the existing national frameworks[179]. An EU official commented drily that the effort to complete

---

[178] The Italian position appear to have made its acceptance of RTSE and EDIS conditional on sovereign debt mutualization, well beyond what Germany and other so-called frugal countries were prepared to consider and also arguably beyond what could be envisaged without treaty change. This echoed a previous episode in 2016: James Politi and Jim Brunsden, 'Italy would block EU bank insurance plan, *Financial Times*, 18 February 2016, https://www.ft.com/content/711dff5c-d63e-11e5-969e-9d801cf5e15b.

[179] Eurogroup statement on the future of the Banking Union, 16 June 2022, https://www.consilium.europa.eu/en/press/press-releases/2022/06/16/eurogroup-statement-on-the-future-of-the-banking-union-of-16-june-2022/.

the banking union was *"certainly not dead, it's taking a nap for a little while"*[180].

At a public event a week after the Eurogroup fiasco, several key policymakers commented on the setback, with a range of opinions on how close an agreement had been. SRB Chair Elke König said *"we have been fairly close to moving the first step into EDIS,"* while John Berrigan, the seniormost European Commission career official on financial services policy, commented that *"we tried to identify all the remaining steps in the banking union, tried to approach it in a holistic way – but it has not worked. [...] It was a heroic effort by the President of the Eurogroup, but it simply wasn't possible to overcome the many obstacles"*[181].

The Eurogroup statement of 16 June 2022 further read: *"we have agreed that, as an immediate step, work on the Banking Union should focus on strengthening the common framework for bank crisis management and national deposit guarantee schemes (CMDI framework). Subsequently, we will review the state of the Banking Union and identify in a consensual manner possible further measures with regard to the other outstanding elements to strengthen and complete the Banking Union".* The latter sentence was a euphemistic confirmation that no discussion of either European deposit insurance or RTSE would restart in the near future. The Eurogroup's mandate on CMDI did not, at this stage, include an ambition to integrate deposit insurance at the European level, only to better coordinate existing national deposit insurance with resolution mechanisms. This political constraint, however, was bound

---

180   Huw Jones, 'EU banking union 'not dead, just napping', says EU official', *Reuters*, 14 June 2022, https://www.reuters.com/business/finance/eu-banking-union-not-dead-just-napping-says-eu-official-2022-06-14/.

181   SRB and ECB Joint Conference, Brussels, 23 June 2022, https://www.srb.europa.eu/en/content/srb-ecb-2022 (conference video).

to create policy challenges of its own. At the same June 2022 conference panel, Berrigan noted soberly: *"What we will discover is that everything in banking union is a bit connected to everything else, so when you make this* [CMDI] *step forward, you're going to find that elements are not there that you would like to have there, and I think EDIS is one of those elements we will find that would be very useful to have if you are trying to build a fully consistent crisis management framework."*

Still, after due consultations, the European Commission on 18 April 2023 published a proposal for CMDI legislation, going some way to address the diagnosed shortcomings of BRRD. Among other things, the proposal introduced:

1. Flexibility for national deposit guarantee schemes to finance the acquisition (*"purchase and assumption"*) of a bank in resolution by another (sound) bank without automatic losses being imposed on other claimants, if that is found to be less costly than the failing bank's liquidation and payout to individual insured depositors (*"least-cost principle"*)[182];
2. Equalisation of all deposits' seniority in resolution above that of other

---

182 Specifically, the CMDI proposal stipulates that financial support from a national deposit guarantee scheme for a purchase and assumption transaction (aimed at protecting depositors under the least cost principle) would not count under the condition, set in the pre-existing version of BRRD, that at least 8 percent of a bank's own funds and eligible liabilities shall be bailed in before any use of public funds such as resolution funds, eg the SRF. That 8 percent condition has been widely criticised as too rigid in situations of systemic crisis, not least by the IMF. It did not result from an in-depth policy development process, but was the outcome of an *ad-hoc* political compromise during late stages of the legislative process on BRRD in late June 2013 (Enoch *et al*, 2013, page 237, point 4). In May 2014, the 8 percent condition was subsequently enshrined in the previously mentioned Inter-Governmental Agreement on the SRF (Recital 17 and Article 9); that text's revision requires unanimity of the member states, implying that the 8 percent condition is harder to modify than other provisions of the BRRD. The CMDI proposal is a way to sidestep this challenge; conversely, it may add credibility to the proposition that liabilities other than deposits would be bailed in.

liabilities, a feature that has existed for some time in the United States and is known there as *"general depositor preference"*[183];

3. A signal that medium-sized banks found to be failing or likely to fail shall receive a positive public interest assessment, or in other words, that resolution would be 'for the many not just the few', in a reversal of the SRB's prior pronouncements[184];

4. A provision to facilitate the transformation of euro-area subsidiaries into branches, by transferring the past payments into the corresponding national deposit guarantee scheme from the host to the home country[185].

---

183 General depositor preference, in conjunction with the least-cost principle, facilitates purchase and assumption transactions in comparison to the present situation in the EU in which insured deposits have preferred status to other retail deposits, which in turn rank higher than other uninsured deposits. This is because, under general depositor preference, the deposit insurer (standing for the insured depositors) loses as much as other depositors, whereas it loses less than them if insured deposits rank higher. (Much also depends on how exactly the least cost principle is formulated and interpreted in practice.) Also, general depositor preference establishes a lower ranking for all liabilities other than deposits, whereas some EU countries currently have the more senior of these (eg senior unsecured debt) rank equally as uninsured deposits. For that reason, general depositor preference is opposed by some banks which claim that it would raise their funding costs. As put succinctly by former FDIC Chair Sheila Bair in a 2013 article in response to the euro area's ostensibly suboptimal response to the Cyprus crisis: *"A claims priority is not hard to construct. Here's how we do it in the US: equity gets wiped out first, followed by junior debt, senior debt, and deposits above the insurance limits. Insured depositors always get paid with losses covered out of reserves built from insurance premiums paid by the industry. We don't protect bondholders for two very good reasons: 1) there is no insurance program for them and they shouldn't get a free ride and 2) they are mostly sophisticated institutions that should be exercising market discipline and a bank's health before deciding to buy its debt"*. Sheila Bair, 'It's time for a European FDIC', *Fortune*, 20 March 2013, https://fortune.com/2013/03/20/sheila-bair-its-time-for-a-european-fdic/.

184 Arguably this is not much of a reform since, as noted above, the implementation of the BRRD in Denmark has already resulted in a positive interest assessment even for very small banks; it would, however, allow the SRB to change its stance without losing face.

185 This would entail changes to Article 14(3) of the Deposit Guarantee Schemes Directive, as advocated publicly by the chair of the ECB Supervisory Board (Enria, 2021). It would be logical, because deposits in a subsidiary are insured by the host country scheme, while deposits in a branch are insured in the home country (that of the parent entity).

The last measure appears to have been rejected outright early in the negotiation. The rest of the package has undergone some legislative discussion, but at the time of writing appears unlikely to be adopted in its entirety – and even partial adoption will most probably not be enacted until 2025 at the earliest, given the EU election cycle in 2024. If the CMDI package is adopted without too many alterations, it may (depending on the fine print) represent an improvement on the status quo, but in any event will not bring fundamental change in terms of addressing the bank-sovereign vicious circle since it leaves the financial responsibility for deposit insurance – and therefore the core of the public safety net for failing banks – at national level.

In December 2023, the deadline passed for a 'fully operational' backstop to the SRF, as had been committed to ten years earlier by finance ministers in the Eurogroup. That backstop, as formulated in June 2019, would be provided by the ESM and is subject to modifications of the ESM Treaty[186]. These treaty amendments have been ratified by all banking union countries except for Italy, with no clarity at time of writing on when the Italian ratification deadlock may be resolved, if at all[187]. Leaving aside the ongoing CMDI discussion, then, the legislative achievements of the 2019-2024 EU parliamentary term in the area of banking reform are limited to the adoption of legislation implementing the last elements of the Basel III accord, albeit not in a compliant

---

186 Details are on the reform section of the ESM website; see https://www.esm.europa.eu/about-esm/esm-reform.
187 See Giuseppe Fonte and Angelo Amante, 'Italy parliament rejects ESM reform, irking Brussels', *Reuters*, 21 December 2023, https://www.reuters.com/world/europe/italian-coalition-parties-vote-against-esm-reform-partl-committee-2023-12-21/.

manner[188], and a technical fix to the BRRD known as the 'daisy chain' legislation[189]. The updating or termination of the 2013 communication on state aid in the banking sector, a response to the crisis context of the time that is evidently no longer relevant, is another action that is long overdue but had not been taken at the time of writing.

In sum, the two pledges made by European Commission President von der Leyen at the start of her term, a European deposit insurance scheme and a backstop to the SRF, have not been realised. There is no change on sovereign exposures or on liquidity in resolution. The main banking union-related legislative proposal made during the term, on CMDI, came late, is limited in scope, and remains far from being finally agreed.

Explaining the deadlock

The lack of progress in nearly a decade of active negotiations may appear puzzling, given the rhetorical support given regularly by nearly all the relevant national political leaders and senior policymakers to the mantra of completing the banking union and breaking the bank-sovereign

---

188 See for example Farah Khalique, 'EU looks set for significant Basel III deviations', *Banking Risk and Regulation*, 3 March 2023, https://www.bankingriskandregulation.com/eu-looks-set-for-significant-basel-iii-deviations/. The final adoption of the package was announced on 30 May 2024; see Council of the EU press release, 'Basel III reforms: new EU rules to increase banks' resilience to economic shocks', https://www.consilium.europa.eu/en/press/press-releases/2024/05/30/basel-iii-reforms-new-eu-rules-to-increase-banks-resilience-to-economic-shocks/.

189 Regulation (EU) 2022/2036, with modifications finally adopted on 26 March 2024. See Council of the EU press release, 'Daisy Chains: Council adopts directive on indirect subscription chains', https://www.consilium.europa.eu/en/press/press-releases/2024/03/26/council-adopts-directive-on-indirect-subscription-chains/.

vicious circle[190]. It cannot be explained only by reluctance to share risks: there have been a number of examples of Europe-wide risk- or cost-sharing that arguably go beyond what is being discussed in relation to banks. Probably the most spectacular is the NextGenerationEU programme decided in mid-2020 in response to the COVID-19 pandemic. In reality, the fundamental need to share risks to ensure the resilience and long-term survival of the euro area is well understood by most participants. The survival of the euro is a genuine, broadly-shared objective among them, not least because of the consistently high public support for the single currency in every member state[191]. Instead, a number of other elements appear to have contributed to the stalemate.

First, heavy historical legacies result in extreme reluctance on the part of some national governments to let go of the idea of a national banking sector. That idea, of course, has been revealed by the 2011-2012 episode of crisis as in tension with the euro's very existence, in addition to being at odds with the EU internal market framework. It also has much less real substance than in the past, an evolution that has been evidently accelerated by the implementation of European banking supervision. The difficulty of introducing RTSE reform, of course, has much to do with the view of domestic banks as pliable to moral suasion to finance national (or sub-national) debt, often referred to as their positive response to the proverbial phone call to bid in a sovereign-bond auction if market demand is insufficient. While the actual importance of that moral suasion mechanism in sovereign-bond markets is open to debate, there is no question

---

190 In March 2024, the Eurogroup once again stated that it *"remains committed to strengthening and completing the Banking Union in a holistic manner"*; see 'Statement of the Eurogroup in inclusive format on the future of Capital Markets Union', 11 March 2024, https://www.consilium.europa.eu/en/press/press-releases/2024/03/11/statement-of-the-eurogroup-in-inclusive-format-on-the-future-of-capital-markets-union/.

191 As regularly documented, among other sources, by Eurobarometer data; see https://europa.eu/eurobarometer/surveys/detail/2981.

that national debt management offices are wary of any RTSE options, including in euro-area countries generally viewed as financially strong.

More broadly, the view that domestic companies are there to serve the domestic interest – which is one definition of economic nationalism – is particularly entrenched with respect to the banking sector. A corollary is the propensity of so-called host countries, namely those in which much of the domestic banking sector is majority-owned by non-domestic banking groups, to 'ringfence' local subsidiaries and keep them under various forms of control by the national authorities – even though, once again, a major instrument of such control has been lost in the transition to European banking supervision[192]. The chair of a large European bank thus candidly observed that "*it cannot be denied that national regulators and supervisors have played a major role* [in the failure to achieve European banking sector integration], *by maintaining – and in certain instances even raising – the barriers for cross-border activity*" (Bini Smaghi, 2024). That such thinking is at odds with the treaty-based EU single market is not enough, to say the least, to lead to its disappearance. Banking nationalism and national financial repression remain prominent in the way many European policymakers think about their economies and financial systems, and represent major obstacles to the completion of banking union.

Second, there remains significant diversity in terms of approaches to moral hazard in bank crisis resolution – in simplistic terms, bail-in or bail-out. These differences between EU countries are driven by history but also by differences in current banking sector structures, business models and relationships between banks and public life, not least at

---

192   The legal instruments used by authorities for such ringfencing vary across cases, and are typically not publicly observable. They appear to include macroprudential mandates, deposit insurance frameworks and occasional direct instructions in blatant infringement of the EU internal market framework.

the local level. In Italy, 'bail-in' (in English) is used near-colloquially and with a heavy negative connotation[193], even though the only cases so far have been losses imposed only on junior creditors – many of whom, to be sure, were unwitting victims of mis-selling by their banks. In Denmark, by contrast, bail-in has been implemented repeatedly and without generating turmoil, not only on junior creditors but also on senior ones and even uninsured depositors, albeit only in cases of comparatively small banks so far. In Germany, national authorities have warned frequently against moral hazard in EU-level legislative discussions. But the German public and policymaking community have displayed a high tolerance for bailouts of domestic public banks, as illustrated by HSH Nordbank or Nord/LB in recent years, and even of private-sector banks such as Düsseldorfer Hypothekenbank, which was rescued at high cost in 2015 by the commercial banks' own deposit guarantee scheme (*Einlagesicherungsfonds*, technically a private-sector fund but mutualised across all commercial banks). The aspiration to shield taxpayers from the consequences of banking crises, which has been central to discourses about banking union and BRRD, appears to be more aligned in some EU countries than in others with the actual preferences of leaders and public opinion, as revealed in the experience of crises. In principle, the SRB may bridge these differences by imposing a consistent approach, but as described above, it is for now only one of many public-sector participants in bank crisis management and resolution.

Third, the completion of banking union has found little active support

---

193 See for example Lorenzo Borga and Gabriele Guzzi, 'Monti o Renzi: chi ha voluto il bail-in?', *lavoce.info*, 6 December 2017, https://lavoce.info/archives/50053/monti-renzi-voluto-bail/.

so far from the banking sector itself[194]. This is somewhat surprising, because some banks, including among the larger ones that have most heft in policy debates, would certainly benefit from it, even though others might not. That the potential beneficiaries do not advocate completion of banking union echoes some past eras, as recorded in chapter 2. But it stands in contrast to others, for example when Deutsche Bank vocally supported more integrated European banking sector policies in the early 2000s. Part of the reason may be that banks are reluctant to deviate from strongly held views of host-country authorities, but that may not provide a full explanation. It cannot be ruled out that an element of nostalgia for the earlier era of closer relationships between supervised entities and public supervisors at the national level might play a role.

Banks' attitudes may also reflect trade-offs related to special advantages embedded in the *status quo*. For example, under the applicable EU legislation, French banks have secured lower deposit insurance requirements and fees than those in any other EU member state, an advantage that could be eroded in the transition to an integrated European deposit insurance system[195].

Finally, there has arguably been an element of bad luck, in contrast to the propitious alignment of circumstances that enabled the birth

---

194 Jacques de Larosière candidly described this reality in a conversation with Andrea Enria (minutes 16-25) at the Fifth ECB Forum on Banking Supervision, 30 November 2023, available at https://www.bankingsupervision.europa.eu/press/conferences/html/20231130_5th_ECB_Forum_Banking_supervision.en.html.

195 The French national deposit guarantee scheme is only pre-funded to cover 0.5 percent of deposits, whereas the ratio is at least 0.8 percent in all other member states (see EBA, https://www.eba.europa.eu/activities/single-rulebook/regulatory-activities/depositor-protection/deposit-guarantee-schemes-data and Tümmler, 2022, pages 1563-1564). The European Commission granted this derogation in line with applicable EU law because the French banking sector is concentrated among a small number of very large banks, including four of the top five banks in the euro area by total assets at end-2022 (based on *The Banker* database). In an integrated system, the European Commission's simulations suggest the ratio might be set at 0.6 percent across the board, implying a manageable increase for French banks but a reduction in their corresponding comparative advantage.

of European banking supervision. At various points, at least some participants in negotiations to complete banking union felt they were gathering momentum, when an unforeseen event suddenly brought them to a halt, eg the disruptive Italian general election outcome in March 2018, the COVID-19 lockdown two years later and the full-scale Russian invasion of Ukraine in February 2022. As ever, there has been much inertia, bad faith, defensiveness and turf protection among many of the participants.

The picture is not entirely bleak, however. There has been progress, if not in terms of decision-making, at least in shared knowledge and insight. The long years of negotiations can be viewed as a collective learning process, bringing better awareness of the trade-offs in the consideration of policy options. Two important examples are evident from the sequence of events: the recognition that resolution and deposit insurance must be addressed as a single challenge, as embedded in the acronym CMDI; and the apparent shift, in the RTSE discussion, from an emphasis on highly procyclical regulatory capital charges based on sovereign credit risk, to an acyclical focus on plain concentration risk, with the option of sovereign concentration charges as described above.

The opposition to any RTSE remains unquestionably strong in some member states, and appears to have been the main cause of the June 2022 collapse of negotiations on banking union. But one often-neglected impact of sovereign concentration charges would be to widen the pool of potential buyers of the debt of all member states, as a mechanical effect of the reduction in exposure concentration. Banks from outside a given euro-area country, which never much considered buying that country's debt, might consider it more than in the past. This offsetting effect could be substantial but is difficult to predict, and inherently conservative national debt-management offices are reluctant to take it into account.

Other aspects of the emphasis on national control and ringfencing are rationalised by the argument that, should a bank (or a banking group's subsidiary) fail in the future, the national budget may be on the hook – an argument that is, in some countries more than others, reinforced by cynicism about the plausibility of bail-in in a future real crisis situation. From that standpoint, an outright transfer from national to European level of all instruments of the safety net for banks, including but not limited to deposit insurance, would facilitate an agreement on the removal of ringfencing options, making euro-area banks genuinely 'European in life and European in death', to paraphrase an oft-quoted saying[196]. As Enria once put it, *"as long as deposit insurance remains national, Member States will have an incentive to ring-fence their banking sectors. This is why we need to finalise the banking union by establishing a European deposit insurance scheme"* (Enria, 2020a). Even a fully integrated European deposit insurance system, however, would certainly not bring a final end to all facets of nostalgic attachment to instruments of national government control of the domestic banking sector.

The concrete implementation of reforms mostly decided in 2012-2013 has gradually eroded the potency of at least some of the obstacles to the completion of banking union, as listed here. Most tangibly, of course, the soundness and resilience of the euro-area banking sector has been much strengthened, in large part thanks to European banking supervision. Improved banking-sector soundness makes most scenarios of systemic banking crisis, let alone of a reactivation of the bank-sovereign vicious circle, much more remote than they were a decade ago. Not only have most banks' capital ratios gone up, but the reliability of capital calculations has been strengthened and additional buffers (minimum requirements for own funds and eligible liabilities in the jargon of the BRRD, set by the SRB for significant euro-area banks) have continued to rise as well. The risk that

---

[196] The quip that *"financial institutions may be global in life, but they are national in death"* was originally coined by Huertas (2009).

giant holes may be discovered, not just in a single bank but in most banks of a given country, let alone across the euro area, was a perceived menace that was prominent in discourse about 'risk reduction' throughout the 2010s, but is less plausible now.

Even so, no event has occurred yet that would force a serious consideration of completing the banking union at the level of heads of state and government, and there is no tangible prospect of breaking the current deadlock in the immediate near term. Veteran EU negotiator Thomas Wieser channelled a widely held opinion by saying in 2022, with reference to the banking union: "*I don't think it will be completed absent a financial sector crisis, which is not on the horizon for now*"[197].

---

197   Tim Gwynn Jones, 'In the Room' podcast, December 2022, https://uk-podcasts.co.uk/podcast/in-the-room-1/ (see also Berès, 2022).

6 EUROPE'S CHOICE: PROCRASTINATE OR ANTICIPATE

Europe's banking union, though unfinished, is an achievement that was widely believed to be beyond reach, until the euro-area crisis made it indispensable. European Investment Bank President Philippe Maystadt, a former Belgian finance minister and seasoned observer of EU policymaking, expressed what was a dominant view at the time when he wrote in 2007 that "*it is probably not realistic (at least in the foreseeable future) to expect an agreement on the creation of an EU* [banking] *supervisor*" (Maes, 2007, page 10). Even after two years of systemic crisis, the report of the high-level group on financial supervision chaired by Jacques de Larosière, while noting the comprehensive failure of national banking supervisors, still concluded that: "*While the Group supports an extended role for the ECB in macro-prudential oversight* […], *it does not support any role for the ECB for micro-prudential supervision*" (Larosière, 2009, pages 43-44). Larosière later clarified that the group "*did not have the majority needed to move in the direction of a single supervisory mechanism*" and that he personally viewed European banking supervision positively[198].

Not only has European banking supervision been created, but,

---

198 Conversation between Andrea Enria and Jacques de Larosière (minute 12) at the Fifth ECB Forum on Banking Supervision, 30 November 2023, available at https://www.bankingsupervision.europa.eu/press/conferences/html/20231130_5th_ECB_Forum_Banking_supervision.en.html.

as indicated in chapter 4, it has established a solid track record of effectiveness and independence. More broadly, the banking union in its current state has greatly increased the euro area's resilience[199]. It has broken new grounds in terms of European-level executive capacity under EU law[200]. It represents a notable example of the EU's ability to introduce and implement radical reform, and has in turn inspired other policy integration projects: for anti-money laundering supervision with the adoption of EU legislation to create a European AML Authority[201], and potentially in matters of energy policy, for which the banking union precedent has been explicitly invoked by successive European Council presidents in response to Russian aggression[202].

Costs of the status quo

Ironically, the success of European banking supervision has also nurtured inertia and complacency on the remaining tasks to tackle

---

199   Niels Thygesen, an experienced Danish and European policymaker, reflected in a 2020 interview that thanks to the banking union and despite its complexity, there had been "*a major reduction of the risks to public finances from exposures to financial sector engagements – arguably the single most significant change in the environment for* [fiscal] *deficits and debt relative to a decade ago*" (Maes and Péters, 2020).

200   ECB official Pedro Gustavo Teixeira (2021) noted: "*The Banking Union is the most advanced form of European integration with a unified system of law, institutions with exclusive competences and enforcement authority subject to judicial review by the Court* [of Justice of the EU] *and accountable to the* [European] *Parliament and the* [EU] *Council.*" He added that the SRM Regulation represents "*the first time that European law provided instruments to an authority* [the SRB] *to affect private property rights.*"

201   The legislation establishing the AML Authority was finally adopted on 30 May 2024; see Council of the EU press release, 'Anti-money laundering: Council adopts package of rules', https://www.consilium.europa.eu/en/press/press-releases/2024/05/30/anti-money-laundering-council-adopts-package-of-rules/.

202   Donald Tusk, 'A united Europe can end Russia's energy stranglehold', *Financial Times*, 21 April 2014, https://www.ft.com/content/91508464-c661-11e3-ba0e-00144feabdc0; and Charles Michel, 'The EU needs a genuine energy union now', *Financial Times*, 6 October 2022, https://www.ft.com/content/04e641ec-b5d8-4dc3-80c6-fde196403f9f.

concentrated sovereign exposures and the crisis management and deposit insurance framework. As highlighted in chapters 3 and 5, Germany's backtracking on its one-time commitment to cross-border risk-sharing, in the form of direct recapitalisation of banks by the ESM, unfolded immediately after the decisive summit of 28-29 June 2012. Successive German governments have since then engaged in consistently delaying tactics under the cover of stated concerns first about *"legacy assets"*, then about *"risk reduction"*[203]. The adept management by European banking supervision of events around the COVID-19 pandemic in 2020 and Russia's full-scale invasion of Ukraine in 2022, and its favourable performance in comparison to US peers in the phase of interest rate raises in 2022-2023, have similarly had the unfortunate side-effect that banking-sector issues have not been prominent on the European political agenda. All the same, European policymakers cannot be satisfied with the banking union *status quo*, for at least four main reasons.

First, the unfinished nature of banking union makes it more difficult to reach several stated EU policy objectives, including capital markets union, open strategic autonomy, the climate transition and a greater international role for the euro. Since the European financial system is overwhelmingly bank-based, the cross-border integration of capital markets is hard to envisage without a foundation of more

---

203 Among numerous examples: Rebecca Christie and Karl Stagno Navarra, 'Merkel Dodges Draghi Call for Clarity With Bank Union Swerve', *Bloomberg*, 18 March 2016, https://www.bloomberg.com/news/articles/2016-03-18/merkel-ducks-draghi-call-for-clarity-dodging-banking-union-move. The 'legacy assets' argument was made in the context of backtracking on ESM direct recapitalisation – namely that the latter should not cover any losses on assets accumulated by banks under national prudential supervision. The joint declaration of the Dutch, Finnish and German finance ministers on 25 September 2012, mentioned in chapter 5, thus stated that *"the ESM can take direct responsibility of problems that occur under the new supervision, but legacy assets should be under the responsibility of national authorities."*

complete banking union, ensuring that financial conditions are not determined by national sovereign creditworthiness. The banking union's incompleteness is also a major obstacle to cross-border bank consolidation, which in turn prevents the emergence of globally leading banks based in the EU.

This view has long been widely held in the investment community. For example, an equity research note published by Goldman Sachs in November 2019 stated in its executive summary that completion of banking union *"would reduce systemic risk, remove barriers to cross-border flow of funds, and introduce incentives for cross-border banking. We see completion* [of the banking union] *as a precondition for the EU to construct a stronger, safer and profitable banking system, able to compete globally"* (Goldman Sachs, 2019; see also Goodhart and Schoenmaker, 2016). As the European banking sector remains fragmented and overbanked, its ability to provide financing for major European projects, including the climate transition, is hampered. One market participant put it vividly: *"Europe's relatively narrow and fragmented financial industry is like a weak financial heart that struggles to pump sufficient capital and liquidity to support healthy European companies and economic growth"*[204]. As for the international role of the euro, it is intimately connected to the creation of a single euro-area financial system, for which the banking union is critical[205].

Second, the incompleteness of banking union makes it doubtful that the EU can operationalise its vision of private-sector liability in the banking sector, as theoretically enshrined in the BRRD – in other words,

---

204   Rebecca Patterson, 'Europe's financial sector is a drag', *Financial Times*, 1 February, 2024, https://www.ft.com/content/68ca6eb3-082f-4bea-b05e-741c4a214b40.
205   See for example *The Economist*, 'The international role of the euro', 24 June 2021, https://www.economist.com/finance-and-economics/2021/06/24/the-international-role-of-the-euro.

bail-in not bailouts. As detailed in the previous chapter, several euro-area countries, most prominently Germany and Italy, have creatively used the leeway offered to them by the current EU crisis-management framework to use public money in cases of bank distress, especially in high-profile cases that triggered recourse to banking nationalism. Bail-in is never easy and, in some scenarios of system-wide fragility, raises legitimate questions about financial stability (eg Geithner, 2014). But the EU should at least be able to reach a comparable level of market discipline to that which exists currently in the United States, even after the sorry episode of Silicon Valley Bank and Signature Bank in March 2023. In the European context, that is essentially impossible as long as national authorities retain a key role in bank crisis management. The *status quo* thus nurtures both moral hazard and, in the event of renewed taxpayer-funded bailouts, the prospect of political disillusionment.

Third, the lingering possibility of a revived bank-sovereign vicious circle, as existed at the peak of the euro-area crisis in 2011-2012, remains a fundamental vulnerability of Europe's monetary union. Fears of a revival of that 'doom loop' played a central role in the weeks immediately following the COVID-19 shock in mid-March 2020, both in terms of rising market turmoil and of the decisive policy response. That response, the NextGenerationEU programme heralded in May 2020 and confirmed in July 2020, involves large-scale EU borrowing over several years to finance the recovery plans of the countries most affected by the fight against the pandemic. While that outcome was highly constructive, the episode once again underlined the fragility of the euro-area construct as long as banking risk remains tightly bound to sovereign credit risk. The incompleteness of the banking union may again encourage the consideration of tail scenarios of euro-area break-up, or pricing of redenomination risk, in future situations of elevated financial stress, in turn contributing to a spiral of financial fragmentation.

Fourth, the *status quo* may result in political frictions that could lead to a policy movement backwards, potentially reversing some or all of the achievements described in this volume. In particular, the spending of national public money to address future banking crises could be attributed, fairly or not, to flaws in European banking supervision, in line with a counterfactual narrative that national authorities would have performed better (as in the fictional scenario of Lascelles, 1996). This would be the flipside of the powerful morality tale that Germany advanced in 2012 to backtrack on ESM direct recapitalisation, with its insistence that German taxpayers should not support the cost of working out legacy assets in other countries: the expense of addressing past failures of national supervision should not be mutualised at European level. Conversely, a view could emerge in some future crisis scenarios that spending of national public money following lapses in European supervision is intolerable, and that the response should be to renationalise supervision. Such scenarios do not appear likely right now, but they could represent a material risk to European financial stability and sustainability. Now that control of the banking sector has been successfully established at European level, the German mantra of aligning liability and control actually calls for the mutualisation of the public safety net to ensure financial stability.

Danièle Nouy put it succinctly, shortly before the end of her term as the first chair of the ECB's Supervisory Board: "*The weaknesses revealed by the crisis triggered the euro area's journey towards a banking union and its decision 'to cross a river.' We have left national supervision and resolution behind but we have not yet reached the other side. We are now in the middle of the river and that is not a good place to be when the flood comes. We have to make it safely to the other side*" (Nouy, 2018).

What it would take

What would it take, in Nouy's words, to make it safely to the other side – or, using an expression that has already appeared repeatedly in this text, to complete the banking union? The above analysis suggests the following two main building blocks:

- An overhaul of the public safety net for the banking sector that would make it fully integrated, meaning all decisions on bank crisis management and resolution would be centralised in a single European agency along similar lines to the FDIC in the United States;
- A change to the EU capital requirements framework intruding gradual capital charges for concentrated sovereign exposures above a certain threshold, or sovereign concentration charges[206].

The 'Euro-FDIC' would presumably be a reformed and renamed version of the SRB[207], relying on at least the resources currently available in the SRF and in the national deposit-guarantee schemes[208]. National authorities should have no role left after the end of the inevitable transition period[209], to avoid perpetuation of the bank-sovereign vicious

---

206 The author's own recommendations for that are sketched in Véron (2017); no event since has suggested a different design or calibration. The IMF (2020) advocated a similar concept.
207 The agency's name should change because the general public should be able to immediately understand its role in circumstances of emergency. The Federal Deposit Insurance Corporation does what its name suggest; by contrast, what a Single Resolution Board is supposed to do is obscure to anyone who is not an expert in the matter.
208 As already mentioned in chapter 5, the SRF and national deposit guarantee scheme together amounted to around €125 billion as of 2023, more than the FDIC's Deposit Insurance Fund.
209 Of course, the need for local bodies in charge of resolution and deposit insurance would remain, presumably one in each banking-union country. Such bodies might take over the existing teams of national resolution authorities and/or deposit guarantee schemes, but should operate under the exclusive legal authority of the Euro-FDIC. That would make the revised SRM and deposit insurance architecture more centralised than that of European banking supervision, in which important tasks are entrusted to national authorities that

circle and to eliminate any residual justification for national ringfencing of capital and liquidity[210]. Other European-level authorities should only interfere to the extent that additional financial resources may be required in certain extreme crisis situations on top of the Euro-FDIC's own[211]. To accompany the institutional overhaul, the bank regulatory framework would be adjusted to empower the Euro-FDIC to handle all cases of bank failures, including small ones[212], with appropriate incentives to protect depositors but not other claimants on failing banks[213], and with

---

        remain accountable to their country's political authorities. The difference would be in line with the EU principle of subsidiarity – that the EU should only have direct authority on matters that its member states cannot address effectively. In a monetary union, the protection of deposits and systemic financial stability would be one such matter.

210   With the full integration of the national resolution authorities into the Euro-FDIC, the current distinction at the SRB between 'plenary' and 'executive' sessions would disappear, since autonomous national resolution authorities would no longer exist. The existing format of the SRB's permanent board (six members, of which five vote in decisions) would presumably be well-suited for the governance of the Euro-FDIC.

211   Namely, the ESM and/or EU Council could be involved in managing a backstop complementing the own resources of the Euro-FDIC, as is the case with Orderly Liquidation Authority in the United States (Klein, 2017). In addition, all financial transactions of the Euro-FDIC should be unambiguously exempt from state aid control since they would not create distortions within the European internal market.

212   In this, the reform would go further than the European Commission's 2023 proposal for CMDI and would essentially extend the previously described Danish stance to the euro area. A corollary would be that there would be no direct need for further harmonisation of national bank insolvency law, since all bank failures would be handled through the resolution process, and the BRRD principle of 'no creditor worse off' in resolution than in national insolvency would thus become obsolete. An important benefit of extending the authority of the Euro-FDIC to all cases of small bank failures would be to create a gradually expanding set of individual cases (since small bank failures are naturally more frequent than those of large banks), with the advantage of increasing predictability (with more precedents) and also of generating a skills base of concrete experience within the agency.

213   In other words, retaining the general depositor preference as proposed by the European Commission in its CMDI text in 2023, with a definition of the 'least-cost test' as rigorous as that which exists in the United States.

provisions to remove the possibility of national ringfencing[214].

This proposed policy package is not novel; it echoes recommendations made in the past decade by multiple observers[215], and incorporates elements discussed by EU member states in 2021-2022, as recounted in the previous chapter. It is liable to criticism for being either too much or too little, which must be weighed carefully.

The too-much critique generally takes the form of asserting that the second element (sovereign concentration charges), a form of RTSE, is unnecessary and potentially destabilising, and that only the first (Euro-FDIC with fully integrated deposit insurance) shall be necessary to complete the banking union. This critique, however, ignores the risk that national governments may leverage the shared European-level safety net, even if that is limited to deposits, to their individual advantage, by applying moral suasion on banks to buy their debt. In other words, sovereign concentration charges are needed in a completed banking union as a pre-emptive measure against national financial repression.

The too-little critique asserts that more progress towards fiscal union is needed as a precondition for completing the banking union, with a reference to European safe assets often used as code for further fiscal policy mutualisation[216]. There is no question that a reform which would entail the permanent issuance of EU debt at scale would greatly facilitate

---

214 In a fully integrated deposit-insurance scheme, of course, the transformation of national subsidiaries of cross-border banking groups into branches, within the euro area, would no longer be impeded as currently, as described by Enria (2021).

215 Two such sets of recommendations, to which the author contributed, were Bénassy-Quéré *et al* (2018) and Beck *et al* (2022). Others included Restoy *et al* (2020) and, albeit only in outline, the conclusion of Tröger and Kotovskaia (2022).

216 This stance was adopted by the European Commission in a 2017 reflection paper: *"A European safe asset would be a new financial instrument for the common issuance of debt [...] Changing the regulatory treatment of sovereign bonds is another issue under discussion to loosen the bank-sovereign loop [...] To take both measures forward, a joint political decision on both aspects would be needed"* (European Commission, 2017, pages 22-23).

the completion of banking union, and arguably make RTSE measures (such as sovereign concentration charges) redundant, since banks would be able to buy EU-level debt that is intrinsically devoid of home bias. The relevant question is, rather, whether completion of the banking union without further fiscal union, along the lines sketched above, would be an improvement on the status quo. In terms of impact on sovereign financing, its net impact would not represent an intrinsic risk for sovereign debt market stability (Pisani-Ferry and Zettelmeyer, 2018). The additional market discipline introduced by sovereign concentration charges would actually have a stabilising effect, since it would represent a disincentive against fiscal drift that the treaty-enshrined EU Stability and Growth Pact, even after multiple reforms, has proved to be unable to provide[217]. The mutualisation of the crisis-intervention framework would clearly be stabilising, as it would be designed not to foster moral hazard.

A separate question is about how much quasi-fiscal backstopping is needed to make an integrated European crisis-management and deposit-insurance framework sustainable. There can be no definitive answer to that question, as all national crisis-management frameworks include an element of incompleteness and time inconsistency. In the United States, the backstop provided to the FDIC is also limited and fuzzy, and it has been a constant policy of the FDIC over multiple crises to not test the boundaries of its possible financial resources[218]. Of course, if European banking

---

217 For example, Luis Garicano, 'The EU's new fiscal rules are not fit for purpose', *Financial Times*, 8 January 2024, https://www.ft.com/content/2ce3860e-b2c9-4579-9600-8b424b014f94.
218 The FDIC has multiple financing options, but its ability to borrow is not unlimited (Ellis, 2013). Under a 2012 rule following the Dodd-Frank Act of 2010 granting it orderly liquidation authority over systemically important financial companies, the FDIC can issue debt up to a maximum obligation limitation proportional to the size of the entity in liquidation. The obligations issued by the FDIC within these limits benefit, under legislation enacted in 1989, from the *"full faith and credit"* of the United States, namely they have the same credit risk as US federal debt.

supervision remains reasonably effective, such boundaries will not be tested in Europe either, even in scenarios of severe financial turmoil[219].

Another key question, about feasibility rather than desirability, is whether the suggested actions can be implemented without prior changes to the EU treaties. Sovereign concentration charges would be well within the scope of the precedent provided by EU internal market legislation on bank capital requirements. The legal architecture of a European deposit-insurance scheme and Euro-FDIC would be identical to that which is already in place for the SRM, only more effective[220].

A politically important matter is how the new system would be articulated with respect to the idiosyncratic IPSs that play such significant roles in Germany and Austria. The straightforward solution would be to transfer their mandatory deposit-guarantee schemes into the new European deposit insurance system managed by the Euro-FDIC[221].

---

219 The reference work on this issue is Carmassi *et al* (2018), which concluded that *"a fully-funded DIF* [Deposit Insurance Fund] *would be sufficient to cover payouts even in a severe banking crisis."*

220 According to a widely held view (eg Teixeira, 2020, page 245), severe limits to autonomous SRB decision-making result from the 1958 *Meroni* jurisprudence of the Court of Justice of the EU (available at https://eur-lex.europa.eu/legal-content/EN/TXT/?uri=CELEX-%3A61956CJ0009). The actual constraints resulting from Meroni remain debated among legal scholars, however (see eg Tröger and Kotovskaia, 2022, page 3, footnote 5). The ESM providing a backstop to the new integrated crisis management and deposit insurance system would entail amendments to the ESM Treaty along similar lines as those attempted for the SRF backstop, and, similarly, ratification by all EU countries.

221 The German cooperative banking group, Austrian Savings Bank Group and Austrian Raiffeisen cooperative banking group have established deposit guarantee schemes under separate entities following the EU Deposit Guarantee Scheme Directive of 2014, respectively the *BVR Institutssicherung GmbH* (BVR-ISG, established 2015), the *Sparkassen-Haftungs GmbH* (recognised as deposit guarantee scheme in 2019) and the *Österreichische Raiffeisen-Sicherungseinrichtung eGen* (ÖRS, established 2021). In the German savings bank groups (*Sparkassen-Finanzgruppe*), the deposit guarantee scheme is currently integrated with the IPS, but there is no fundamental reason why it could not be separated into a different entity along similar lines as has been done in the three other cases. (Also, for a few years in the 2010s, the Austrian Raiffeisen Group joined the general Austrian deposit insurance scheme, before

Similarly in the German commercial banking sector, the statutory deposit-guarantee scheme (*Entschädigungseinrichtung deutscher Banken*, EdB) would become part of the integrated European system, while the 'top-up' additional insurance (*Einlagensicherungsfonds*) could retain its current autonomy[222].

In terms of the balance between bail-in and bail-out, the most compelling model – though by no means uncontroversial in the EU context, as we have seen – remains that of the FDIC, namely a high level of protection for all depositors, buttressed by general depositor preference, and essentially no public protection for other liability holders, with requirements for capital and liability buffers at least maintained at their current levels in Europe[223]. A more restrictive state-aid control framework should ensure that protections for liabilities other than deposits are not introduced at the national level, which would create intra-banking union competitive distortions.

It must be noted that the proposals sketched above stop well short of creating a seamless single market for banking services, in which all important national idiosyncrasies would be erased. Major differences would remain in taxation, consumer protection, corporate and personal insolvency law, housing finance and pension finance, to name just a few

---

re-establishing its own in 2021, further demonstrating the practical feasibility of transitions from one system to another.) The problems associated with having the deposit guarantee scheme embedded in an IPS are detailed in Huizinga (2022, page 18). On proposals for IPS reform in Germany more generally, see eg Haselmann *et al* (2022).

222 Like most existing deposit guarantee schemes, the European system would of course entail a risk-based calculation of deposit-insurance fees adjusted based on a risk assessment of each insured bank. Setting the principles for such calculations would surely be an important component of the legislative negotiations on the reforms proposed here.

223 These "*minimum requirements for own funds and eligible liability*" are what was missing in Silicon Valley Bank and Signature Bank in March 2023. Their established availability in Europe should reduce the scope for 'systemic risk exemption' compared to the recent US experience.

policy areas that have significant influence on bank business models and financial-sector structures. Completing the banking union, as envisaged here, is a more modest endeavour than a uniform banking market, as it is focused on breaking the linkages between bank credit and sovereign credit. It can be achieved fairly rapidly if the political will is there to make it happen. By contrast, a single market in banking services is a very distant prospect in any scenario (Beck *et al*, 2022).

The suggested reforms, even if implemented in full, would certainly not put an immediate end to reflexes of banking nationalism. There would still be political resistance to cross-border acquisitions in the banking sector, for example. But it would become much harder for individual countries to block these on prudential considerations. Nor could national authorities invoke financial-stability concerns to force banks to ringfence their capital or liquidity along national borders inside the banking union, or veto the conversion of subsidiaries into branches within cross-border banking groups.

There is no articulated, consistent policy narrative that would provide for the EU a compelling alternative to the completion of banking union. All political leaders pay lip service to the latter, even when engaging in stalling tactics. In that respect, what remains to be done to complete the banking union may be viewed as less politically difficult than what has already been achieved since June 2012, because it does not require nearly as big a leap of imagination. In that sense, there is cause for optimism.

Jean Monnet's oft-quoted sentence, *"I have always believed that Europe would be built through crises, and that it would be the sum of their solutions"*, describes accurately the start of banking union in 2012-2014 (Monnet, 1978, page 417). There are counterexamples, however, including the creation of the euro itself. The euro's starting point, the Delors Committee of 1988-1989, was not a rushed response to emergency, but a reasoned effort based on sound economic analysis of the need for a single currency to sustain the single market project, even though unexpected circumstances later played a major role in making a reality of the ECB and the euro. One wishes for the EU that its banking union might be completed as part of a similarly forward-thinking endeavour.

REFERENCES

Altavilla, C., M. Pagano and S. Simonelli (2017) 'Bank Exposures and Sovereign Stress Transmission', *Review of Finance* 2017: 1-37

Angeloni, I. (2020) *Beyond the Pandemic: Reviving Europe's Banking Union*, London: CEPR

Aslund, A. (2010) *The Last Shall Be the First: The East European Financial Crisis*, Washington DC: Peterson Institute for International Economics

Barker, A. and G. Parker (2012) 'Finance: A union to bank on', *Financial Times Big Read*, 18 June

Bassani, G. (2020) 'The Centralisation of Prudential Supervision in the Euroarea: The Emergence of a New 'Conventional Wisdom' and the Establishment of the SSM', *European Business Law Review* 31(6): 1001-1022

Bastasin, C. (2015) *Saving Europe: Anatomy of a Dream*, Washington DC: Brookings Press

Baudino, P.M. and F. Restoy (2023) 'The 2008–14 banking crisis in Spain', *FSI Crisis Management Series* No 4, Basel: Financial Stability Institute

Bayoumi, T. (2017) *Unfinished Business: The Unexplored Causes of the Financial Crisis and the Lessons Yet to be Learned*, New Haven: Yale University Press

BCBS (2017) 'The regulatory treatment of sovereign exposures', *Discussion paper*, December, Basel Committee on Banking Supervision

Beck, T., J.-P. Krahnen, P. Martin, F.C. Mayer, J. Pisani-Ferry, T. Tröger, N. Véron, B. Weder di Mauro and J. Zettelmeyer (2022) 'Completing the banking union: Economic requirements and legal conditions', *Policy Insight* No. 119, Centre for Economic Policy Research

Bénassy-Quéré, A., M. Brunnermeier, H. Enderlein, E. Farhi, M. Fratzscher, C. Fuest, P-O. Gourinchas, P. Martin, J. Pisani-Ferry, H. Rey, I. Schnabel, N. Véron, B. Weder di Mauro and J. Zettelmeyer (2018) 'Reconciling risk sharing with market discipline: A constructive approach to euro area reform', *Policy Insight* No. 91, Centre for Economic Policy Research

Berès, P. (2022) 'The banking union, a real priority! Badly shared?' *Revue* 134, Confrontations Europe

van den Berg, C. (2005) *The Making of the Statute of the European System of Central Banks: An Application of Checks and Balances*, Amsterdam: Dutch University Press

Berg, J. and S.U. Lind (2023) 'Why there is no need to stray from the original ideas behind the Bank Recovery and Resolution Directive', *SUERF Policy Note* No. 306, Société Universitaire Européenne de Recherches Financières

Bini Smaghi, L. (2011) 'Tommaso Padoa-Schioppa – economist, policymaker, citizen in search of European unity', speech to the European University Institute, 28 January, available at https://www.bis.org/review/r110131f.pdf

Bini Smaghi, L. (2024) 'Banking Union, Ten years After', *IEP@BU Policy Brief*, January, Institute for European Policymaking at Bocconi University

Bolton, P. and O. Jeanne (2011) 'Sovereign Default Risk and Bank Fragility in Financially Integrated Economies', *IMF Economic Review* 59(2): 162-194, International Monetary Fund

Busch, D. and G. Ferrarini (eds) (2015) *European Banking Union*, Oxford University Press

Calomiris, C. (1999) 'The Impending Collapse of the European Monetary Union', *Cato Journal*, 1 January

Calomiris, C. and S. Haber (2014) *Fragile by Design: The Political Origins of Banking Crises and Scarce Credit*, Princeton University Press

Cameron, R. (1967) *Banking in the Early Stages of Industrialization: A Study in Comparative Economic History*, Oxford University Press

Carmassi, J., S. Dobkowitz, J. Evrard, L. Parisi, A. Silva and M. Wedow (2018) 'Completing the Banking Union with a European Deposit Insurance Scheme: who is afraid of cross-subsidisation?' *Occasional Paper Series* 208, European Central Bank

Coeuré, B. (2013) 'The Single Resolution Mechanism: Why it is needed', speech to the International Capital Market Association Annual General Meeting in Copenhagen, 23 May, available at https://www.ecb.europa.eu/press/key/date/2013/html/sp130523.en.html

Constâncio, V. (2011) 'A European solution for crisis management and bank resolution', speech to the ECB Conference on Bank Resolution, Stockholm, 14 November, available at https://www.ecb.europa.eu/press/key/date/2011/html/sp111114.en.html

Constâncio, V. (2018) 'Completing the Odyssean journey of the European monetary union', speech to the ECB Colloquium on the Future of Central Banking, Frankfurt, 17 May, available at https://www.ecb.europa.eu/press/key/date/2018/html/ecb.sp180517.en.html

Council of the EU (2014) *Banking Union, Relevant European Council conclusions*, General Secretariat of the Council, available at https://www.consilium.europa.eu/media/21548/20141020-banking_union_-_relevant_ec_conclusions.pdf

CRS (2020) *Bank Supervision by Federal Regulators: Overview and Policy Issues*, Washington DC: Congressional Research Service, December

Dahlgren, S., R. Himino, F. Restoy and C. Rogers (2023) *Assessment of the European Central Bank's Supervisory Review and Evaluation Process*, Report by the Expert Group to the Chair of the Supervisory Board of the ECB, Frankfurt: European Central Bank

Danmarks Nationalbank (2021) 'Consistent recovery and resolution of small and large banks in Europe', *Analysis*, 30 June

Decressin, J., H. Faruqee and W. Fonteyne (eds) (2007) *Integrating Europe's Financial Markets*, Washington DC: International Monetary Fund

Delors, J. (1989) *Report on economic and monetary union in the European Community*, Committee for the Study of Economic and Monetary Union, 12 April

De Rynck, S. (2014) 'Changing Banking Supervision in the Eurozone: the ECB as a Policy Entrepreneur', *Bruges Political Research Papers* No. 38, College of Europe

De Rynck, S. (2015) 'Banking on a union: the politics of changing eurozone banking supervision', *Journal of European Public Policy* 23(1): 119-135

De Rynck, S. (2017) 'Banking Union', in N. Zahariadis and L. Buonanno (eds) *The Routledge Handbook of European Public Policy*, Taylor & Francis

Drach, A. (2019) 'A globalization laboratory: European banking regulation and global capitalism in the 1970s and early 1980s'. *European Review of History* 26(4), March.

Drach, A. (2020) 'Reluctant Europeans? British and French Commercial Banks and the Common Market in Banking (1977-1992)', *Enterprise & Society* 21(3): 768-798

Drach, A. (2021) 'An early form of European champions? Banking clubs between European integration and global banking (1960s-1990s)', *Business History* 66(1): 287-310

Draghi, M. (2012) 'Introductory statement' to the Committee on Economic and Monetary Affairs of the European Parliament, Brussels, 25 April, available at https://www.bis.org/review/r120426b.pdf

Draghi, M. (2013) 'Stable euro, strong Europe', speech to the *Wirtschaftstag* in Berlin, 25 June, available at https://www.bis.org/review/r130626a.pdf

Draghi, M. (2019) 'Policymaking, responsibility and uncertainty', Speech at Università Cattolica, Milan, 21 October, available at https://www.bis.org/review/r191011d.htm

ECA (2016) 'Single Supervisory Mechanism – Good start but further improvements needed', *Special Report* 29, European Court of Auditors

ECA (2023) 'EU supervision of banks' credit risk', *Special Report* 12, European Court of Auditors

ECB (2001) 'The role of central banks in prudential supervision', European Central Bank, available at https://www.ecb.europa.eu/pub/pdf/other/prudentialsupcbrole_en.pdf

ECB (2008) *Simulating Financial Instability*, Conference on stress testing and financial crisis simulation exercises, 12-13 July 2007, European Central Bank

ECB (2013) 'Opinion of the European Central Bank on a proposal for a Council regulation conferring specific tasks on the European Central Bank concerning policies relating to the prudential supervision of credit institutions and a proposal for a regulation of the European Parliament and of the Council amending Regulation (EU) No 1093/2010 establishing a European Supervisory Authority (European Banking Authority)', 2013/C 30/05

ECB (2020) *Risk report on less significant institutions*, European Central Bank, January

ECB (2021) *ECB Banking Supervision: SSM Supervisory Priorities for 2022-2024*, European Central Bank, available at https://www.bankingsupervision.europa.eu/banking/priorities/pdf/ssm.supervisory_priorities2022~0f890c6b70.en.pdf

ECB (2022a) *ECB Annual Report on supervisory activities 2021*, European Central Bank

ECB (2022b) *Administrative Board of Review: Eight years of experience reviewing ECB supervisory decisions*, European Central Bank, available at https://www.bankingsupervision.europa.eu/ecb/pub/pdf/ssm.aborreview202212~ce9fb4e503.en.pdf

ECB (2022c) *LSI Supervision Report 2022*, European Central Bank

ECB (2023) *ECB Annual Report on supervisory activities 2022*, European Central Bank

ECB (2024) *ECB Annual Report on supervisory activities 2023*, European Central Bank

Eichengreen, B. (1993) 'European Monetary Unification, *Journal of Economic Literature* XXXI: 1321-1357

Ellis, D. (2013) 'Deposit Insurance Funding: Assuring Confidence', *Staff Paper*, November, Federal Deposit Insurance Corporation

Enderlein, H. and E. Rubio (2014) '25 years after the Delors Report: what lessons for economic and monetary union?' *Policy Paper* 109, Notre Europe/Jacques Delors Institute

Enoch, C., L. Everaert, T. Tressel and J. Zhou (2013) *From Fragmentation to Financial Integration in Europe*, International Monetary Fund

Enria, A. (2020a) 'The road towards a truly European single market', speech to the 5th SSM and European Banking Federation Boardroom Dialogue, 30 January, available at https://www.bankingsupervision.europa.eu/press/speeches/date/2020/html/ssm.sp200130~f5b1d43756.en.html

Enria, A. (2020b) 'A European supervisory system: from vision to reality', speech to the ECB colloquium in commemoration of Tommaso Padoa-Schioppa, 18 December, available at https://www.bankingsupervision.europa.eu/press/speeches/date/2020/html/ssm.sp201218~21c950cc63.en.html

Enria, A. (2021) 'How can we make the most of an incomplete banking union?' speech to the Eurofi Financial Forum in Ljubljana, 9 September, available at https://www.bankingsupervision.europa.eu/press/speeches/date/2021/html/ssm.sp210909~18c3f8d609.en.html

Enria, A. (2023a) 'A new stage for European banking supervision', speech to the 22nd Handelsblatt Annual Conference on Banking Supervision, 28 March, available at https://www.bankingsupervision.europa.eu/press/speeches/date/2023/html/ssm.sp230328~1797047d39.en.html

Enria, A. (2023b) 'Twenty years of (bumpy) progress: harmonising supervisory reporting in the EU', speech to the ECB Supervisory Reporting Conference 2023, 26 April, https://www.bankingsupervision.europa.eu/press/speeches/date/2023/html/ssm.sp230426~008d00b7a8.en.html

Enria, A., A. Farkas and L.J. Overby (2016) 'Sovereign Risk: Black Swans and White Elephants', *European Economy*, 8 July

Epstein, R. and M. Rhodes (2014) 'International in Life, National in Death? Banking Nationalism on the Road to Banking Union', *Working Paper* No. 61, Freie Universität Berlin Kolleg-Forschergruppe

ESM (2019) *Safeguarding the euro in times of crisis*, European Stability Mechanism

ESRB (2015) *ESRB report on the regulatory treatment of sovereign exposures*, European Systemic Risk Board

European Commission (1999) 'Implementing the Framework for Financial Markets: Action Plan', COM(1999) 232

European Commission (2017) 'Reflection Paper on the Deepening of the Economic and Monetary Union', COM(2017) 291

European Commission (2017b) 'Commission staff working document accompanying the Report from the Commission to the European Parliament and the Council on the Single Supervisory Mechanism established pursuant to Regulation (EU) No 1024/2013', SWD(2017) 336 final

European Commission (2017c) 'Communication on completing the Banking Union', COM(2017) 592 final

European Commission (2023) 'Report on the Single Supervisory Mechanism established pursuant to Regulation (EU) No 1024/2013', COM(2023) 212 final

FDIC (2017) *Crisis and Response: An FDIC History, 2008-2013*, Federal Deposit Insurance Corporation

FDIC (2023) *Options for Deposit Insurance Reform*, Federal Deposit Insurance Corporation

FDIC (2024) *Overview of Resolution Under Title II of the Dodd-Frank Act*, Federal Deposit Insurance Corporation

Financial Crisis Inquiry Commission (2011) *The Financial Crisis Inquiry Report: Financial Report of the National Commission on the Causes of the Financial and Economic Crisis in the United States*, New York: Public Affairs

Fonteyne, W., W. Bossu, L. Cortavarria, A. Giustiniani, A. Gullo, D. Hardy and S. Kerr (2010) 'Crisis Management and Resolution for a European Banking System', *Working Paper* WP/10/70, International Monetary Fund

FRB (2023) *Review of the Federal Reserve's Supervision and Regulation of Silicon Valley Bank*, Federal Reserve Board

Frudiger, J. (2022) 'The Netherlands and the negotiation of the Economic and Monetary Union: An 'actor-centered' analysis of the Dutch EMU negotiations and Council Presidency of 1991', mimeo, University of Leiden

GCEE (2011) *Annual Report 2011: Assume Responsibility for Europe*, German Council of Economic Experts

Geithner, T. (2014) *Stress Test: Reflections on Financial Crises*, New York: Crown Publishers

Gelpern, A. and N. Véron (2018) 'The Long Road to a US Banking Union: Lessons for Europe', in J.F. Kirkegaard and A.S. Posen (eds) *Lessons for EU Integration from US History*, Peterson Institute for International Economics

Gelpern, A. and N. Véron (2019) *An Effective Regime for Non-viable Banks: US Experience and Considerations for EU Reform*, Study requested by the ECON committee, European Parliament

Giovannini, A. (1993) 'Central banking in a monetary union: reflections on the proposed statute of the European Central Bank', *Carnegie-Rochester Conference Series on Public Policy* 38: 191-230

Glöckler, G., J. Lindner and M. Salines (2017) 'Explaining the sudden creation of a banking supervisor for the euro area', *Journal of European Public Policy* 24(8): 1135-1153

Goldstein, M. (2017) *Banking's Final Exam: Stress Testing and Bank-Capital Reform*, Washington DC: Peterson Institute for International Economics

Goldman Sachs (2019) 'Bank Union Completion: Light at the end of the tunnel; positive', Goldman Sachs Equity Research, 8 November

Gong, C. (2020) 'The 2012 private sector involvement in Greece', *Discussion Paper Series* 11, European Stability Mechanism

Goodhart, C. (2011) *The Basel Committee on Banking Supervision: A History of the Early Years 1974-1997*, Cambridge University Press

Goodhart, C. and D. Schoenmaker (2016) 'The Global Investment Banks are Now All Becoming American: Does that Matter for Europeans?' *Journal of Financial Regulation* 2(2)

Government of Sweden (2019) 'Sverige och bankunionen', English summary of SOU 2019:52, Swedish Government Inquiries

Grant, C. (2015) '25 Years On: How the Euro's Architects Erred', *Insight*, 5 November, Centre for European Reform

Haselmann, R., J.P. Krahnen, T. Tröger and M. Wahrenburg (2022) *Institutional Protection Schemes: What are their differences, strengths, weaknesses, and track records?* In-depth analysis request by the ECON Committee, European Parliament

Haselmann, R., S. Singla and V. Vig (2022) 'Supranational Supervision', *LawFin Working Paper* No. 50, Foundations of Law and Finance

Hellwig, M. (2014) 'Yes Virginia, There is a European Banking Union! But It May Not Make Your Wishes Come True', *Preprints of the Max Planck Institute for Research on Collective Goods*, August, Max Planck Society

Hellwig, M. (2018) 'Germany and the Financial Crisis 2007-2017', mimeo, available at https://www.bundesbank.de/resource/blob/759000/c7f985a2adbdf1c54ba385406a4b5294/mL/2018-06-15-stockholm-06-paper-hellwig-data.pdf

Högenauer, A.-L. (2023) 'The ECB as a banking supervisor: transparent compared to what?' *Journal of European Integration* 45(1): 121-137

Hollande, F. (2018) *Les leçons du pouvoir*, Paris: Stock

Howarth, D. and L. Quaglia (2014) 'The Steep Road to European Banking Union: Constructing the Single Resolution Mechanism', *Journal of Common Market Studies* s1(52)

Huertas, T.F. (2009) 'The Rationale for and Limits of Bank Supervision', mimeo, available at https://www.researchgate.net/publication/242359838_The_Rationale_for_and_Limits_of_Bank_Supervision

Huizinga, H. (2022) *Institutional Protection Schemes - What are their differences, strengths, weaknesses, and track records?* In-depth analysis request by the ECON Committee, European Parliament

IMF (1998) *Selected Issues in Mature Financial Systems: EMU, Banking System Performance, and Supervision and Regulation*, International Monetary Fund

IMF (2011) 'Luxembourg: Financial System Stability Assessment—Update', *Country Report* No. 11/148, International Monetary Fund

IMF (2020) 'Italy: Financial System Stability Assessment', *Country Report* No. 2020/081, International Monetary Fund

Italianer, A. (1993) 'Mastering Maastricht: EMU issues and how they were settled', in K. Greschmann (ed) *Economic and Monetary Union: Implications for National Policy-makers*, Maastricht: European Institute of Public Administration

James, H. (2012a) 'Lessons for the Euro from History', mimeo, Julis-Rabinowitz Center for Public Policy and Finance Conference, European Crisis: Historical Parallels and Economic Lessons, 19 April, available at https://jrc.princeton.edu/sites/g/files/toruqf2471/files/jrcppf_2012_-_james_-_paper.pdf

James, H. (2012b) *Making the European Monetary Union: The Role of the Committee of Central Bank Governors and the Origins of the European Central Bank*, Cambridge MA and London: Harvard University Press

Jonung, L. and E. Drea (2009) 'The euro: It can't happen, It's a bad idea, It won't last. US economists on the EMU, 1989 – 2002', *Economic Papers* 395, European Economy, European Commission

Judge, K. (2023) 'Written Testimony before the hearing A Failure of Supervision: Bank Failures and The San Francisco Federal Reserve', U.S. House of Representatives Oversight Committee, Subcommittee on Health Care and Financial Services, 24 May

Juncker, J.-C. (2014) *A New Start for Europe: My Agenda for Jobs, Growth, Fairness and Democratic Change*, European Commission, 15 July

Juncker, J.-C. (2015) *The Five Presidents' Report: Completing Europe's Economic and Monetary Union*, European Commission

Kindleberger, C.P. (1993) *A Financial History of Western Europe (Second Edition)*, Oxford University Press

Klein, A. (2017) 'A primer on Dodd-Frank's Orderly Liquidation Authority', *Commentary*, 5 June, Brookings

Lagarde, C. (2011) 'Global Risks Are Rising, But There Is a Path to Recovery', remarks at the Jackson Hole Economic Symposium, 27 August, available at https://www.imf.org/en/News/Articles/2015/09/28/04/53/sp082711

Lagarde, C. (2012) 'Global Challenges in 2012', speech in Berlin, 23 January, available at https://www.imf.org/en/News/Articles/2015/09/28/04/53/sp012312

Lamfalussy, A. (2001) *Final Report of the Committee of Wise Men on the Regulation of European Securities Markets*, 15 February

Lamfalussy, A. (2013) *Le sage de l'euro : entretien avec Christophe Lamfalussy, Ivo Maes et Sabine Péters*, Brussels: Racine

Larosière, J. de (2009) *The High-Level Group on Financial Supervision in the EU, chaired by Jacques de Larosière: Report*, 25 February

Lascelles, D. (1996) *The Crash of 2003: An EMU fairy tale*, London: Centre for the Study of Financial Innovation

Lastra, R. (1992) 'The Independence of the European System of Central Banks', *Harvard International Law Journal* 33(2)

Lehmann, A. and N. Véron (2021) *Tailoring prudential policy to bank size: The application of proportionality in the US and euro area*, In-depth analysis request by the ECON Committee, European Parliament

von der Leyen, U. (2019) *A Union that strives for more: My agenda for Europe*, European Commission, 16 July

Lo Schiavo, G. (ed) (2019) *The European Banking Union and the Role of Law*, Edward Elgar

Maes, I. (2007) *Half a century of European financial integration*, Brussels: Mercatorfonds

Maes, I. (ed) (2017) *Alexandre Lamfalussy: Selected Essays*, Budapest: Hungarian National Bank

Maes, I. and S. Péters (2020) 'A Dane in the making of European Monetary Union – A conversation with Niels Thygesen', *Working Paper* No. 382, National Bank of Belgium

Maes, I. and S. Péters (2021) 'Interview of Jacques de Larosière: In search of a better world financial order', *History of Economic Thought and Policy* 2-2021

Magnus, M., C. Dias and K. Grigaite (2022) 'Public hearing with Elke König, Chair of the Single Resolution Board', *Briefing*, July, European Parliament

Majnoni D'Intignano, G., A. Dal Santo and M. Maltese (2020) 'The FDIC bank crisis management experience: lessons for the EU Banking Union', *Notes on Financial Stability and Supervision* No. 22, Banca d'Italia

Mersch, Y. (2018) 'The limits of central bank financing in resolution', speech at Goethe University, Frankfurt, 30 January, available at https://www.ecb.europa.eu/press/key/date/2018/html/ecb.sp180130.en.html

Middelaar, L. van (2019) *Alarums and Excursions: Improvising Politics on the European Stage*, Agenda Publishing

Mody, A. (2009) 'From Bear Stearns to Anglo Irish: How Eurozone Sovereign Spreads Related to Financial Sector Vulnerability', *Working Paper* WP/09/108, International Monetary Fund

Mody, A. and D. Sandri (2011) 'The Eurozone Crisis: How Banks and Sovereigns Came to be Joined at the Hip', *Working Paper* WP/11/269, International Monetary Fund

Monnet, J. (1978) *Memoirs* (translated by Richard Mayne), Garden City NY: Doubleday

Mourlon-Druol, E. (2016) 'Banking Union in Historical Perspective: The Initiative of the European Commission in the 1960s–1970s', *Journal of Common Market Studies* 54(4)

Mourlon-Druol, E. (2025) *Federal Anathema: How European Policmakers Shelved Economic Union in the Making of the Euro*, Ithaca NY: Cornell University Press, forthcoming

Newell, J.R. (2023) 'Written testimony before the hearing *A Failure of Supervision: Bank Failures and The San Francisco Federal Reserve*', U.S. House of Representatives Oversight Committee, Subcommittee on Health Care and Financial Services

Nielsen, B. and S. Smeets (2018) 'The role of the EU institutions in establishing the banking union. Collaborative leadership in the EMU reform process', *Journal of European Public Policy* 25(9)

Nouy, D. (2018) 'Risk reduction and risk sharing – two sides of the same coin', speech to the Financial Stability Conference, Berlin, 31 October, available at https://www.bankingsupervision.europa.eu/press/speeches/date/2018/html/ssm.sp181031.en.html

Otero-Iglesias, M., S. Royo and F. Steinberg (2016) 'The Spanish financial crisis: Lessons for the European Banking Union', *Informe* 20, Elcano Royal Institute, Madrid

Padoa-Schioppa, T. (1999) 'EMU and Banking Supervision', lecture at the London School of Economics, 24 February, available at https://www.ecb.europa.eu/press/key/date/1999/html/sp990224.en.html

Padoa-Schioppa, T. (2004) 'How to deal with emerging pan-European financial institutions?' speech to the Conference on Supervisory Convergence in The Hague, 3 November, available at https://www.ecb.europa.eu/press/key/date/2004/html/sp041103.en.html

PIIE (2023) 'What works and what doesn't in the EU bank resolution framework', recorded event, 25 October, available at https://www.piie.com/events/what-works-and-what-doesnt-eu-bank-resolution-framework

Pisani-Ferry, J. and J. Zettelmeyer (2018) 'Could the 7+7 report's proposals destabilise the euro? A response to Guido Tabellini', *VoxEU*, 20 August

Rehn, O. (2020) *Walking the Highwire: Rebalancing the European Economy in Crisis*, Palgrave Macmillan

Restoy, F. (2019) 'How to improve crisis management in the banking union: a European FDIC?' speech to the CIRSF Annual International Conference, Lisbon, 4 July, available at https://www.bis.org/speeches/sp190715.pdf

Restoy, F., R. Vrbaski and R. Walters (2020) 'Bank failure management in the European banking union: What's wrong and how to fix it', *Occasional Paper* No. 15, Financial Stability Institute

Rogers, I. (2017) 'Ivan Rogers on Cameron's Brexit referendum', *Politico*, 24 November

Schäfer, D. (2017) *Explaining the Creation of the EU Banking Union: The Interplay between Interests and Ideas*, London School of Economics and Political Science

Schnabel, I. and N. Véron (2018) 'Breaking the stalemate on European deposit insurance', *VoxEU*, 7 April

Schoenmaker, D. and N. Véron (eds) (2016) *European Banking Supervision: The First Eighteen Months*, Blueprint Series 25, Bruegel

Schüler, M. (2004) 'Integrated Financial Supervision in Germany', *ZEW Discussion Paper* No. 04-35, Centre for European Economic Research

Smits, R. (1997) *The European Central Bank, Institutional Aspects*, Kluwer Law International

SRB (2019) *Public Interest Assessment: SRB Approach*, Single Resolution Board, 3 July

SRB (2023) *Small and medium-sized banks: resolution planning and crisis management report for less significant institutions in 2022 and 2023*, Single Resolution Board, October

Swaim, S. and M. Wessels (1991) 'Lessons learned from recent U.S. banking experience', Paper presented at the Sixth Annual Symposium of the Foundation for Research in International Banking and Finance, Berlin, 3 May, available at https://www.gao.gov/assets/143801.pdf

Taos, T. (2021) 'Why not have one, neutral and integrated safety net system for resolution and deposit guarantee?' *SRB Blog*, 28 October, Single Resolution Board

Teixeira, P.G. (2020) *The Legal History of the European Banking Union*, Hart Publishers

Teixeira, P.G. (2021) 'The future of the Banking Union after the pandemic', *RED Revue Européenne du Droit* 3, December

Tooze, A. (2018) *Crashed: How a Decade of Financial Crises Changed the World*, Penguin Books

Tröger, T. (2017) 'Too complex to work: A critical assessment of the bail-in tool under the European bank recovery and resolution regime', *Working Paper* 116, Institute for Monetary and Financial Stability, Goethe University Frankfurt

Tröger, T. and A. Kotovskaia (2022) 'National interests and supranational resolution in the European Banking Union', *SAFE Working Paper* 340, Leibniz Institute for Financial Research SAFE

Tümmler, M. (2022) 'Completing Banking Union? The Role of National Deposit Guarantee Schemes in Shifting Member States' Preferences on the European Deposit Insurance Scheme', *Journal of Common Market Studies* 60(6): 1556-1572

Tuominen, T. (2017) 'The European Banking Union: A Shift in the Internal Market Paradigm?' *Common Market Law Review* 54(5): 1359-1380

Van Rompuy, H. (2011) *Towards a Stronger Economic Union: Interim Report*, European Council, 6 December

Van Rompuy, H. (2012) *Towards a Genuine Economic and Monetary Union*, European Council, 26 June

Van Rompuy, H. (2014a) '4th Annual Tommaso Padoa-Schioppa Lecture', speech to the Brussels Economic Forum, 10 June, available at https://www.consilium.europa.eu/media/25742/143160.pdf

Van Rompuy, H. (2014b) 'Speech at the European Central Bank in Frankfurt on the occasion of the inauguration of the Single Supervisory Mechanism', 20 November, available at https://www.consilium.europa.eu/media/25009/145893.pdf

Véron, N. (2007) 'Is Europe ready for a major banking crisis?' *Policy Brief* 2007/03, Bruegel

Véron, N. (2011) 'Europe must change course on banks', *Bruegel Blog*, 18 December

Véron, N. (2012) 'Is Europe ready for Banking Union?' *Bruegel Blog*, 18 May

Véron, N. (2013) 'Banking Nationalism and the European Crisis', speech to the European Private Equity and Venture Capital Association 30th Anniversary Symposium, 27 June, available at https://www.piie.com/sites/default/files/publications/papers/veron20130627.pdf

Véron, N. (2016) 'The IMF's Role in the Euro Area Crisis: Financial Sector Aspects', *Background Paper* BP/16-02/10, Independent Evaluation Office of the International Monetary Fund

Véron, N. (2017) *Sovereign Concentration Charges: A New Regime for Banks' Sovereign Exposures*, Study requested by the ECON committee, European Parliament

Véron, N. (2019) *Taking Stock of the Single Resolution Board*, In-depth analysis requested by the ECON committee, European Parliament

Vianelli, M. (2022) 'Achieving a Shared Consensus: the Delors Committee and the Relaunch of the EMU Process', *Journal of European Integration History* 28(2)

Vives, X. (1992) 'The supervisory function of the European System of Central Banks, *Giornale degli Economisti e Annali di Economia* 51(9/12): 523-532

Zeitlin, J. (2023) 'Hierarchy, polyarchy, and Experimentalism in EU Banking Regulation: The Single Supervisory Mechanism in Action', *Journal of European Integration* 45(1): 79-101

Zettelmeyer, J. (2011) 'A "bridge to somewhere": Building a comprehensive strategy for resolving the Eurozone debt crisis', *VoxEU*, 24 October

Appendix A: Sample of banks and selected bank-level data summarised in Tables 1 and 2

Banking group	Country	Mid-2016					Mid-2023				
		Total assets (€m)	Tier 1 capital (€m)	Domestic sovereign exposures	Home bias	Tier 1 capital coverage	Total assets (€m)	Tier 1 capital (€m)	Domestic sovereign exposures	Home bias	Tier 1 capital coverage
BAWAG	AT	35,458	2,044	3,973	80%	194%	53,152	3,177	2,798	92%	88%
Erste Group	AT	204,505	13,534	10,496	57%	78%	343,975	24,289	8,808	46%	36%
Raiffeisen Bank International	AT	113,969	7,255	2,412	25%	33%	205,634	17,501	3,526	38%	20%
Raiffeisenbank Oberösterreich	AT	40,541	3,115	2,966	80%	95%	48,937	4,463	1,244	49%	28%
Volksbank Group	AT						29,559	2,192	867	69%	40%
Belfius	BE	188,004	7,523	25,701	82%	342%	163,331	11,204	20,279	90%	181%
Crelan	BE	30,860	949	2,247	36%	237%	54,059	2,162	475	71%	22%
Argenta Bank	BE	38,669	1,713	2,471	68%	144%	53,788	2,673	1,225	56%	46%
KBC Group	BE	265,681	14,568	21,425	57%	147%	338,260	18,558	13,942	49%	75%
Bank of Cyprus	CY	22,680	2,736	509	100%	19%	24,896	1,827	1,002	75%	55%
Hellenic Bank	CY	7,091	679	515	84%	76%	20,063	1,312	962	89%	73%
Aareal Bank	DE	50,925	2,762	6,082	61%	220%	48,898	2,568	2,317	64%	90%
Bayerische Landesbank (BayernLB)	DE	224,296	8,959	34,714	95%	387%	272,990	11,291	28,823	96%	255%
Commerzbank	DE	532,602	26,303	26,734	52%	102%	518,946	28,336	13,876	55%	49%
DekaBank	DE	104,307	4,575	8,567	90%	187%	104,611	6,034	4,217	81%	70%
Deutsche Apotheker- und Ärztebank (Apobank)	DE						51,719	2,612	2,576	100%	99%
Deutsche Bank	DE	1,803,290	56,382	25,767	47%	46%	1,303,004	57,676	8,872	20%	15%
Deutsche Pfandbriefbank (PBB)	DE	67,492	2,663	6,907	34%	259%	49,766	3,072	2,478	22%	81%
DZ Bank	DE	521,354	14,991	32,395	81%	216%	546,447	26,921	18,301	79%	68%

Banking group	Country	Mid-2016					Mid-2023				
		Total assets (€m)	Tier 1 capital (€m)	Domestic sovereign exposures	Home bias	Tier 1 capital coverage	Total assets (€m)	Tier 1 capital (€m)	Domestic sovereign exposures	Home bias	Tier 1 capital coverage
Landesbank Berlin Holding	DE	3,270	3,279	7,968	88%	243%	62,656	2,974	1,017	81%	34%
Hamburg Commercial Bank	DE	90,796	5,803	12,068	89%	208%	30,786	3,061	1,123	91%	37%
HASPA Hamburger Sparkasse	DE						59,218	4,653	7,435	100%	160%
Landesbank Baden-Württemberg (LBBW)	DE	259,693	12,677	26,268	85%	207%	361,406	14,239	11,745	86%	82%
Landesbank Hessen-Thüringen (Helaba)	DE	175,629	7,841	30,500	94%	389%	209,272	9,143	30,334	100%	332%
Münchener Hypothekenbank	DE						54,061	1,955	3,575	91%	183%
Norddeutsche Landesbank (NORD/LB)	DE	179,166	7,987	33,014	87%	413%	111,590	6,014	13,692	91%	228%
Volkswagen Bank	DE	49,126	13,254	1,004	44%	8%	71,776	9,237	1,045	42%	11%
LHV Pank	EE						6,307	478	234	60%	49%
Luminor	EE						15,455	1,429	161	12%	11%
BBVA	ES	746,040	50,364	65,124	83%	129%	736,309	51,316	49,562	77%	97%
Cajamar Cooperative Group	ES						61,975	3,381	6,993	47%	207%
Banco Sabadell	ES	207,891	10,281	19,156	74%	186%	243,432	11,759	26,468	85%	225%
Banco Santander	ES	1,342,907	72,190	51,699	78%	72%	1,765,405	86,485	38,777	60%	45%
Bankinter	ES						110,099	5,198	7,226	72%	139%
CaixaBank	ES						555,027	31,771	79,652	83%	251%
Ibercaja	ES						47,539	2,695	10,867	90%	403%
Kutxabank	ES						63,539	5,285	10,467	100%	198%
Unicaja	ES						96,732	5,048	20,333	73%	403%
Kuntarahoitus (Munifin)	FI						48,377	1,500	15,803	100%	1054%
Nordea	FI	301,107	26,958	3,812	31%	14%	529,356	27,154	743	25%	3%

Banking group	Country	Mid-2016 Total assets (€m)	Mid-2016 Tier 1 capital (€m)	Mid-2016 Domestic sovereign exposures	Mid-2016 Home bias	Mid-2016 Tier 1 capital coverage	Mid-2023 Total assets (€m)	Mid-2023 Tier 1 capital (€m)	Mid-2023 Domestic sovereign exposures	Mid-2023 Home bias	Mid-2023 Tier 1 capital coverage
OP Group	FI	124,899	8,334	1,755	27%	21%	135,494	13,650	2,494	47%	18%
BNP Paribas	FR	2,171,989	78,864	45,653	37%	58%	2,422,259	108,345	42,492	34%	39%
Bpifrance	FR						104,614	25,734	27,048	100%	105%
Crédit Mutuel	FR	738,624	40,747	33,324	80%	82%	956,351	65,187	14,689	77%	23%
Groupe BPCE	FR	1,219,744	54,322	167,575	87%	308%	1,404,732	70,108	195,122	87%	278%
Crédit Agricole	FR	1,770,663	78,943	85,156	76%	108%	1,998,408	112,065	77,804	69%	69%
La Banque Postale	FR						334,841	19,337	93,593	92%	484%
RCI Banque	FR	37,073	3,586	142	38%	4%	62,773	5,465	108	100%	2%
SFIL	FR	85,806	1,376	49,289	87%	3383%	66,947	1,530	45,649	91%	2983%
Société générale	FR	1,460,243	49,754	0	0%	0%	1,431,500	60,995	35,507	72%	58%
Alpha Bank	GR	67,372	8,522	3,645	96%	43%	72,041	4,780	7,268	65%	152%
Eurobank Ergasias	GR	72,652	6,514	3,690	100%	57%	81,521	6,580	5,476	86%	83%
National Bank of Greece	GR	83,917	8,828	10,003	48%	113%	72,849	5,777	11,401	64%	197%
Piraeus Bank	GR	84,727	9,193	2,338	13%	25%	76,983	4,466	8,722	69%	195%
Allied Irish Banks	IE	97,387	9,819	8,535	75%	87%	131,275	10,776	4,538	78%	42%
Bank of Ireland	IE	126,267	7,467	4,056	63%	54%	134,939	8,755	3,795	77%	43%
Banca Mediolanum	IT						40,905	2,717	19,122	100%	704%
Banca Monte dei Paschi di Siena	IT	164,386	9,147	25,259	98%	276%	120,812	7,896	15,994	100%	203%
Banca Popolare di Sondrio	IT	35,623	2,522	7,438	100%	295%	53,948	3,334	9,426	72%	283%
Banco BPM	IT						192,554	9,776	15,440	50%	158%
BPER Banca	IT						143,092	7,602	13,042	80%	172%

Banking group	Country	Mid-2016					Mid-2023				
		Total assets (€m)	Tier 1 capital (€m)	Domestic sovereign exposures	Home bias	Tier 1 capital coverage	Total assets (€m)	Tier 1 capital (€m)	Domestic sovereign exposures	Home bias	Tier 1 capital coverage
Cassa Centrale Banca	IT						91,115	7,662	30,744	87%	401%
Credito Emiliano	IT	37,395	1,737	3,417	63%	197%	56,085	2,927	4,817	73%	165%
FinecoBank	IT						33,816	1,570	6,016	37%	383%
ICCREA Banca	IT						168,240	12,527	59,411	99%	474%
Intesa Sanpaolo	IT	717,292	39,761	59,266	67%	149%	781,961	47,822	42,271	57%	88%
Mediobanca	IT	71,549	6,505	7,038	79%	108%	91,486	8,178	7,364	68%	90%
UniCredit	IT	891,477	45,134	77,208	52%	171%	843,528	54,787	49,994	54%	91%
Banque et Caisse d'Épargne de l'État (Spuerkeess)	LU						56,324	4,822	1,881	58%	39%
Banque Internationale à Luxembourg	LU						30,801	1,598	437	10%	27%
Quintet Private Bank	LU						12,813	680	12	2%	2%
Citadele banka	LV						4,820	391	372	42%	95%
MDB Group	MT	2,791	196	10	4%	5%	4,898	216	0	0%	0%
Bank of Valletta	MT	10,496	553	1,325	77%	239%	14,265	1,057	1,384	46%	131%
ABN AMRO Bank	NL	418,940	18,056	9,789	32%	54%	403,767	22,033	3,009	16%	14%
BNG Bank	NL	163,456	3,669	34,733	83%	947%	128,318	4,413	33,778	84%	765%
Rabobank	NL	686,593	35,070	21,575	81%	62%	630,203	45,297	2,335	40%	5%
de Volksbank	NL	62,589	3,083	1,928	38%	63%	73,028	3,465	775	20%	22%
ING Group	NL	885,659	48,271	15,206	22%	32%	1,029,181	55,277	4,186	9%	8%
Nederlandse Waterschapsbank	NL						75,909	2,237	50,354	100%	2251%
Banco Comercial Português	PT	73,068	4,719	6,373	99%	135%	90,954	6,361	6,536	42%	103%
Caixa Geral de Depósitos	PT	99,355	6,013	14,883	84%	248%	97,313	8,755	8,852	51%	101%

Banking group	Country	Mid-2016						Mid-2023				
		Total assets (€m)	Tier 1 capital (€m)	Domestic sovereign exposures	Home bias	Tier 1 capital coverage		Total assets (€m)	Tier 1 capital (€m)	Domestic sovereign exposures	Home bias	Tier 1 capital coverage
LSF Nani (Novo Banco)	PT	55,291	4,332	1,774	36%	41%		44,151	2,498	4,712	45%	189%
Nova Ljubljanska Banka	SI	11,761	1,280	1,805	78%	141%		24,701	2,269	756	40%	33%
Gorenjska Banka	SI							5,991	912	199	62%	22%

Source: EBA. Note: For readability, individual banks are referred to in this table by their common commercial name, which in some cases differs from that of the consolidated entity listed by the EBA.

www.ingramcontent.com/pod-product-compliance
Lightning Source LLC
LaVergne TN
LVHW061630070526
838199LV00071B/6632